SQUARE PEGS, ROUND HOLES

SQUARE PEGS, ROUND HOLES

Square Pegs, Round Holes

REFLECTIONS UPON THE CROSS-CULTURAL DILEMMA
OF INDIAN SUBCONTINENT DIASPORA

Square Pegs, Round Holes

REFLECTIONS UPON THE CROSS-CULTURAL DILEMMA
OF INDIAN SUBCONTINENT DIASPORA

Jaswant Singh Sachdev, M.D., F.A.A.N.

Horizon Unlimited L.L.C.
Phoenix, Arizona, USA

ISBN No. 978-0-615-20631-8

Jaswant Singh Sachdev, M.D., F.A.A.N
Phoenix, Arizona
email: jaswantsachdev@cox.net

Published in the United States of America by
Horizon Unlimited L.L.C.
Phoenix, Arizona

Manufactured in the United States of America by
Sir Speedy Printing, Tustin
13554 Newport Ave., Tustin CA 92780 • Ph: (562) 881-7430

First Edition

This book is dedicated to 'The Power That Be' for bestowing upon me the gift of an extraordinary mother, 'Bee Ji' who showed me the way to a Truthful Living early-on in my life
and
to my dearest wife Swinderjit, a true source of inspiration and strength. She kept me totally free from all the worries of daily life to pursue my passion to complete this book.

SQUARE PEGS, ROUND HOLES

CONTENTS

Introduction

On a compass, East and West point in opposite directions. Upon settling in the West, an immigrant from the East experiences a similar polarity of cultural differences from medical and health issues to family affairs, from etiquette concerns to language problems, as well as many other matters. So how can one assimilate to a new land without losing one's way?

For a number of years, Dr. Jaswant Singh Sachdev, has written articles for a variety of publications about immigrants integrating in new homelands, providing ideas and insights about adapting to an adopted country while maintaining one's culture. In other words, how one goes about fitting a square peg in a round hole. Square Pegs, Round Holes collects these writings into an anthology that should answer many questions from immigrants as well as those who are native born. Indeed, the opportunity to work on this book smoothed the edges of my understanding about various practices and customs of the East.

If you trace a globe of the world with your hands by moving your left hand to the West and your right hand to the East, eventually your hands will meet and reach common ground. The material in Square Pegs, Round Holes likewise shows each of us how to merge East and West respectfully, peacefully, and harmoniously, no matter where one was born or where one lives now.

Wendy Ring,
Masters in Fine Arts and Creative Writing

11

Preface

Introducing the contents of a book to a prospective reader is indeed a Herculean task for it requires a serious discipline from the author. First of all, there always is a concern that what is being stated in the preface must be in complete sync with the contents that are to follow. At the same time, the author needs to create and maintain a certain degree of curiosity so that the reader turns the pages beyond the introduction of the book which, in fact, happens to be the ultimate intent of the writer.

My initial exposure to the West, like many other teenagers in India of yester-years, had been through books and magazines. However, my true contact with Western culture took place for the first time in 1972 when I landed on the shores of America. The Statue of Liberty in the city of New York, where I first arrived from India, has always stood ready to embrace immigrants from all corners of the world irrespective of their faiths, cultures and countries. The Big Apple, as New York City is popularly known, has indeed been allowing everyone to take a bite of it.

Those who understood the Western culture and those who found it overbearing or intimidating were all able to adjust in this metro, albeit to a variable degree. Most lived happily side by side in its multi-faceted and multi-cultural plethora. The easy availability of public transportation, the presence of ethnically diverse diaspora, the variety of the ethnic restaurants and foods as well as the religious institutions of every faith, made new entrants of each ethnicity feel at home in the Big Apple. The same turned out to be true in the formative years of my living in the West.

After finishing my training in Neurology in 1976 at New York Medical College, it was my turn to say good-bye to the city of New York and move onward like so many ahead of me. I wanted to find a place where I could raise my family away from the hustle and bustle of a big city. My search finally led me to an oasis in the desert of the Southwestern United States, a place known to the world as Phoenix, Arizona but I adopted it as my permanent home. Obviously, Phoenix in those days was a small sleepy town, not that well known. But being from India, I was no different than my people when it came to taking a plunge in unknown territories. In fact, the light-hearted joke penned below explains these typical Indian characteristics rather clearly:-

"In the late sixties, when the first man from the U.S., Mr. Neil Armstrong, landed on moon, he was literally surprised to find an Indian, Mr. Singh, a boisterous turbaned Sikh, holding a garland of flowers to welcome and treat him to a hearty lunch at his Indian restaurant. A Punjabi owner of a corner gas station humbly provided him with all the gas. Later in the evening, an Indian movie, 'Mother India,' from Bollywood was screened in honor of Mr. Armstrong. Another Indian of Gujarati descent, Mr. Patel, offered him a free night stay at his motel. The next day, he visited a software research lab where a sophisticated program was being developed by many Indians with a majority from South India."

Since my arrival in the U.S., I have been intimately connected with the Indian diaspora while having my full share of American-hood. In fact, I have thoroughly seen, fully lived and deeply felt both cultures from very close quarters. Although my professional career has been entirely devoted to the discipline of Neurology, there always has been a second part of me that yearned to highlight the cultural asymmetries pertaining to the lifestyle of my community in the Western surroundings. Unfortunately, the constraints and demands of my profession didn't leave much time for me to write about this cross-cultural dilemma of the Indian subcontinent diaspora. Yet sincere attempts by our people to adjust in foreign cultures of the West, the way I saw it and understood it, always kept on providing me with enough material that I hoped to write about one day.

Some years ago, when an acquaintance started a local Indian monthly in English, it finally created an outlet for me to use my pen, nay the word processor! The use of the word processor became a major stimulant for me to pursue my suppressed hobby of writing seriously. Slowly and steadily, several local and national ethnic weeklies serving the diaspora of the Indian subcontinent became interested in publishing my articles and thus the material kept on accumulating. Many conversations and emails from my readers finally convinced me to put all this together in the form of a book. With the perseverance and motivation of my wife and several close friends, I felt encouraged enough to ultimately take the initiative.

The subject matters discussed in these articles happen to be the outcome of collective discussions and observations with my friends and readers. Most of the material deals with social behaviors of South Asians, primarily the Indian subcontinent immigrants settled in Western countries. At the same time, given my medical background, it was but natural that some of the articles would point toward medical issues. The members of the diaspora often confront such problems or situations discussed in this book. Those who haven't yet, will, perhaps do so in the future as we move along. Each article is an independent entity in itself, bearing little or no relationship with the others. There is no set pattern and they do not follow any sequence. Some repetition is bound to occur simply because each one of these articles took birth in the grey matter of my brain at a different point in time, some even years apart.

The lifestyles of the immigrants, prior to their arrival in the Western lands, naturally differ in many ways and forms from the cultures, behaviors and attitudes of the indigenous Western people of the host countries. Therefore, first generation Indians, like other past groups of immigrants, go through a process of gradual metamorphosis. A side by side comparison between the two lifestyles of an immigrant, one before and one after the settlement, is the subject matter of some of these writings. Having been at both ends of the spectrum, indeed offered me many unique experiences that I have written about openly and repeatedly. In fact, many readers have often mentioned to me personally that what is being stated in these articles is what they always wished to communicate, but didn't or couldn't.

While we all try our best to be part of the lifestyles of the prevalent cultures, deep within us there always kindles a hope that our religious and cultural identities will not be completely overtaken by the wrath of Western culture. This duality is continuously experienced by all the immigrants, albeit to different degrees. The Westerners, from their point of view, also keep on hoping against hope that the positive features of their indigenous lifestyles will not be entirely overwhelmed or decimated by the onslaught of foreign cultures. Such thought processes end up pulling each group in opposite direction resulting in subtle under surface conflicts. That is why many among us often wish that the struggles we have been through should become known to a wider cross-section of prospective immigrants so that those waiting in line could have a prior understanding of what they are getting into. A tremendous amount of theoretical information is already available to a person new to this culture. Yet when it comes to seeking practical tips, many find themselves at a loss.

Some of the readers might question my objectives in putting together this anthology for they might find it nothing more than unpleasant commentary about the lifestyles and behaviors of the Eastern immigrants. To them, I must humbly remind that my intent here is simply to bring forth and highlight some of our shortcomings that are truly in need of perusal. Nothing will improve or get better if we are not willing to explore as to what went wrong and where and their possible corresponding solutions, notwithstanding that many among us are already aware of our own attitudes and deficiencies. It is human nature to ignore criticism and try to look the other way when people talk about such matters.

At the same time, it needs to be openly and clearly mentioned that the Western culture, with which I have tried to compare our attitudes and behaviors, also possesses its own weaknesses, especially if seen through the cultural prism of the East. No one can or should deny that. But this is not the subject matter of this book and I have not emphasized this angle, although readers will find occasional comments about the lifestyles, cultures and habits of the people of our adopted homelands. I will not hesitate in saying, however, that in no way, shape or form should my articles be construed in making anyone feel that certain-less-than palatable intricacies are unilateral.

I must point out that our ongoing struggle to assimilate in the melting pot should not necessarily translate into justifying that we have to completely de-identity ourselves and lose our cultural identities. Granted, a certain amount of cultural transformation will take place in view of several hurdles that may befall en route. Oftentimes, we will succeed and other times we may not. I personally believe that there is nothing wrong in accepting mid-course social and cultural corrections so long as such corrections do not tread upon the basic principles of one's faith. And in my way of thinking, it is possible and doable.

In many ways, the life of an Eastern immigrant can be compared to that of a "square peg" which requires a forceful push to pass through a "round hole," or the indigenous Western culture. In doing so, bruises are likely to occur but once the edges of the peg are smoothed out somewhat, the passage of the peg through the "round hole" will become easy. In other words, with continuous minor adjustments, the life of people from the East can become wholesome and fruitful. This indeed is the message that many of my articles keep harping on repeatedly and persistently. It was for this reason alone that I have chosen this particular title for this book.

I sincerely pray that the reader, while enjoying this book, will perceive the messages contained therein, in the spirit and intent in which they have been written and certainly not in any other way.

Jaswant Singh Sachdev, M.D., F.A.A.N.
Phoenix, Arizona USA
jaswantsachdev@cox.net

Acknowledgements

There are several individuals who truly deserve my respect and gratitude for putting an extreme degree of effort towards this undertaking. First and foremost, I must thank my life-partner, Swinderjit Kaur Sachdev, who stood by me and kept on encouraging to carry on. Working full time in medical profession in an adopted homeland certainly makes one bankrupt as far the quota of time is concerned. Yet for this hobby of mine, if I were to call it so, Swinderjit made sure that I am kept totally free from all other household obligations so that I could devote my full energies and efforts to this project. Without her total and complete commitment, this book would never have seen the light of the day.

My children, Dr. Mankanwal Singh Sachdev, Dr. Harkanwal Singh Sachdev, Dr. Jasgit Kaur Sachdev, as well as S. Sarbjit Singh and Jaskanwal Kaur all put their selfless efforts in the project both emotionally and otherwise and thus deserve my full gratitude. Equally important are my other family members S. Raminderpal Singh Gulati and Rupinder Kaur Gulati as well as Maneet and Guneet. The innocent love of my little lovely angels - Pia, Chiraag and Hargun - kept me going throughout this endeavor.

I am greatly indebted to Mr. Deke Barker and his wife Darcy Barker, both of whom reviewed the manuscript and guided me in the various facets of this project. Mrs. Juhi Bhalla, a family friend and greatly helpful person, spent long hours in going through each article one by one and for it I am sincerely thankful. My lifelong friend, Mr. Pritam Singh, M.A., of Los Angeles took great pains in helping me get there, where I now happen to be. Pritam was a constant source of motivation and had put a tremendous amount of effort into reading and offering valuable suggestions. Mrs. Amarjit Kaur and Aman were always available for help. To my great luck Gopinder Birak applied her technological expertise with linguistic skills for one final review.

Dr. Shyam Tangri, Dr. Eric Erlbaum and Dr. Venu Gopal, my professional associates, also went through a part of the manuscript and provided guidance. Professor Narinder Singh Kapoor, a childhood friend, world renowned author of Punjabi, a retired Professor and, head of the Department of Journalism and Punjabi at Punjabi University in Patiala, India has been my mentor. He has been graciously translating all my articles for a future Punjabi version of this book. Mr. Darshan Singh Teji, a long time friend always kept on sending his good wishes for the final completion of this project. But above all, it was Mrs.Wendy Ring who arrived at the scene as a true savior. She reviewed the entire manuscript and finally made this project happen. Her introductory comments truly sum up what this book is all about. I will remain greatly indebted to all.

I will not do justice if I ignored the special credit due to Mr. Jayant Dholakia, the owner and publisher of Valley India Times, as well as the editor, Miss Jesal Dholakia. In fact this anthology is the outcome of what has been a regular feature in this highly successful local ethnic monthly since its inception. Thanks, too, to the publishers and editors of several other newspapers including S. Mohinder Singh of the India-Journal, Los Angeles; J.S. Bedi of the India-Post, San Francisco; S. Daljit Singh Sra, the Editor of the Amritsar Times, San Jose. These publications have frequently printed my articles. In fact the list of weeklies and monthlies is too long to enumerate.

Mr. Jagjit Singh, Gurmeet Singh, Hetal Sakaria, Tirthankar Chatterjee and their team of associates at Sir Speedy, my printers in Tustin, California have done a yeoman's job in designing the cover and setting the book in print. The result speaks for itself.

But above all, I remain greatly indebted and thankful to my highly motivated readers who have been continuously encouraging me to put these thoughts together in the form of a book.

J.S.S.

SQUARE PEGS, ROUND HOLES

.

.

1.

Adoption and Biological Parenthood

Sometime back, one of my long time acquaintances casually happened to make this comment, "Although I would like my-thirty-year-old daughter to get married and make me a grandma, I would rather not ask her to do so."

I became somewhat curious, as I couldn't figure out what she meant by this statement. She then went on to tell me that her daughter suffers from an illness that could relapse again and become worse by pregnancy. The acquaintance further added, "My daughter doesn't have to make me a grandma by becoming a natural mother. I would be equally content if she just adopts a baby. For that matter, even a cat will be fine for me, and I have told her so." Her words might have sounded funny at the time, but they made me pause and think about what she had truly meant through her statements.

Having lived in the Western culture for over thirty-five

years, I had a feeling that I understood this culture fairly well. However, she made me realize that this is not exactly true. Could we ever imagine such statements from a woman of Indian origin? It was at this moment that my imagination took me deep into the differences in the thought processes between the people of East and West, especially in relation to marriage and procreation. The Indian subcontinent culture and religions emphasize marriage for each and every individual born on this earth. None of the parents would be happy until they have succeeded in their responsibilities of getting their children, especially the daughters in matrimonial alliances. Since time immemorial, the unmarried grown-up girls in India in many circumstances have been considered a painful burden on the family. Therefore, parents always seem to carry a burning desire to unload them as soon as they reach marriageable age.

Until lately, our culture expected parents to find a match for their daughters and to some extent for their sons, therefore, a candidate's personal feeling and motivation in this regard was not considered important. In view of heavy and at times, unreasonable demands put forth by boy's parents under the garb of a dowry, finding a suitable male match for one's daughter oftentimes became difficult, if not impossible. This difficulty often led girl's parents to bend backward. The match for a daughter didn't have to be rich, handsome, healthy or personally resourceful. A heartbeat was about all that was required in the boy. Throughout this ordeal though, parents of the girl always maintained a hope that the prospective husband and in-laws of their daughter would not keep on bugging and torturing her in seeking additional dowries as time passed by.

God forbid if the girl had any physical handicap or if her parents were unable to pay hefty dowry; in either case, marriage was next to impossible. Yet in Indian culture, life is considered incomplete without matrimonial alliance, therefore, marriage for a girl and for that matter for a boy is a must.

But the story does not end here. The truly painful saga of a married woman in India who cannot conceive begins just after marriage. The day a girl steps into married life in India, the whole focus of her in-laws and other people around her shifts towards the production of children. The parents of the newlyweds in India always encourage the new couple -- and especially the daughter-in-law -- to deliver a male grandchild to them as soon as possible.

If the signs of pregnancy do not appear within a few months or a year after the wedding, the young wife's life, in some circumstances, is turned into a living hell. Each and every available method is adopted to determine her ability to bring another soul, especially male, into this already overpopulated earth. This includes consultation with physicians, with vaids, with wise men, and also with so-called 'psychics' like the ones we are always being bombarded with, in the advertisements on Indian television channels. Every possible magic and ritual is performed to help expedite the process. Until a male child is born, the couple will be encouraged to keep on producing as having a male child is the only way, they think, the progeny could be continued. This can easily be considered one of the causes of the population explosion in India. At times, the problem might lie with the husband, but usually it is the wife who is blamed and considered responsible for lack of producing offspring, especially males.

What is not stated here is that our faiths do not specifically speak against adoption, nor do they oppose adoption where conception is not possible. And yet, adoption is not actively encouraged and not much credence is given to it. At the same time, a lack of cultural and societal encouragement may be the reason that adoption is not considered to be a normal or acceptable way to enjoy the pleasure of raising children, even though it may be the only and the most viable option in some cases.

Western culture has a different belief system, but one fact is clear; the desire to become a mother is equally strong in Western woman as it is in Indian woman. Obviously, she too would prefer to have a natural or 'biologic' child over adoption, much like women of the East. However, if for whatever reason, the woman and her spouse are not able to conceive, they will not regard the situation as the end of the world, nor will their families and friends. And this is where the cultural gap becomes obvious.

The culture of the West believes very strongly that to enjoy a child, it need not be one's natural or 'biologic' child. Adoption is seen as providing an equally good outlet for all of the pent up love. Additionally, the adoption of an orphaned child not only allows the adopting couple to become happy parents, but it also creates a suitable and loving environment for an adopted-orphan child. That is one reason why so many Western families rush to, wherever they can find a child for adoption. Once it becomes obvious that further efforts at producing a natural child are likely to be futile, the prospective parents say good-bye to procrastination and start looking for a child to adopt.

Especially worth noting is the willingness of people in this culture to accept a child of a different race if they are unable to find one of their own, and unwilling to wait for what can be a very long process. In fact, thousands and thousands of dollars are spent in locating a suitable child, even in far-away countries.

By contrast, if an Indian couple finally decides to adopt a child, they first look to their own close families. If it doesn't work out, the best they will settle for will be a child of their own ethnicity. Rarely does one come to know about an Indian looking outside of India for a child to adopt. Another issue that hinders the adoption process among Indian parents, often relates to their built-in desire to adopt a male child. Unfortunately, baby girls are considered a 'responsibility in waiting' that many Indian parents are unwilling to take. In little girls, they end up perceiving the burden of a pending 'dowry' in the near future. Thus it further cuts into the option or process of adoption.

There is a real need for childless Indian couples to consider the option of adoption if they are unable to conceive. Such a failure on their parts prevents them from having an opportunity at the right time to enjoy the pleasures and fruits of parenthood that they were looking for throughout their married life. At the same time, a noble opportunity to change the life of a needy child in providing him or her a permanent home is also lost by not taking this step. Many couples of Indian origin spent their entire married lives waiting in hope that one day God Almighty will answer their prayers. And yet, true prayers could definitely be listened to and answered if, indeed, they were for the goodness of humanity at large. The answers to such prayers may be those many orphaned and/or unwanted children who are available for adoption in various orphanages all around India and in other parts of the world.

Some among the Indian culture may opine that one cannot shower the same level of affection on an adopted child as on a natural child. This belief certainly is neither borne out by scientific explanation, nor by the scrutiny of Western cultural and social attitudes. One may come across random cases here and there, especially in countries like India where some elements of discrimination could exist in the minds of parents of adopted children but this will be more of an exception than the rule.

One has but to look at the love and affection people shower on their 'adopted' pets. Would they give any less love and affection to adopted children? A couple that is unable to procreate but is blessed with the resources to take care of an adopted child needs to go out for adoption by all means and plunge into such an opportunity at the earliest instance.

It is comforting to realize that with world continuously shrinking and turning smaller due to evolution in the information technology, some positive changes in the attitudes and behaviors of people of the Indian subcontinent are becoming more evident. I hope and pray that such rays of hope will keep on enlightening our hearts and minds, thus opening up the closed, dark avenues within us. Adoption of orphaned children, irrespective of their genders, is a right way to go for the couples having difficulty in procreation and must be encouraged. Procrastination and waiting unnecessarily for a miracle to happen is unwise and uncalled for. Adoption is good, noble and consistent with the philosophy of many Eastern faiths and its use, when needed, is something definitely worthy of incorporation and that too, rather sooner than later.

2.
And Tomorrow it Could be Your Child…. or Mine!

Who would not wish to extend a lease on the life of one's son, daughter or a grandchild? And who would want to lose such a precious gift after having been blessed with one? These painful thoughts often make my nights sleepless when I come to know about a child of the Indian subcontinent pedigree losing the game of life simply because no one came forward to offer a small amount of bone marrow that he or she direly needed to survive. Many such children suffering from acute leukemia or other fatal blood illnesses wither away without seeing the light of future days in the absence of available matching donors. This kind of apathy among our people causes ripples in my heart and turns my stomach upside down. I ask myself how it is that we, the people from the Indian subcontinent, who otherwise are willing to donate any amount of money to build and sustain more temples,

31

gurdwaras, mosques and churches, fail miserably when it comes to donating parts of our bodies, parts that will not impair our ability to function perfectly well without. The answer is painfully obvious.

We donate to the places of worship, in part, because of a genuine need, but more often than not we do so to satisfy our egos and out of a belief that by building more religious places, we will be assured a seat in heaven. For some obscure reasons, a gift that can save the life of a helpless child without causing much discomfort to our bodies and pockets is usually not on our agenda. Rarely do we consider that helping a dying child with such a gift of life might assure us of a rather better seat in heaven, perhaps even in the first row, if there were such a thing? Moreover, the spoken and unspoken words of gratitude of the life thus saved will often go a long way in showering lifelong blessings on the donor.

Most people in the West whom we casually write-off as materialistic, stand ready to silently help in finding solutions to ease the pain and suffering of their fellow human beings. They support research by all the available means at their disposal to find new treatments to control illnesses that if left alone could cause havoc. Many rich individuals in Western countries establish or support privately sponsored charitable foundations. Organizations like the American Cancer Society, the American Heart Association, the Parkinson Disease Foundation, the National Multiple Sclerosis Foundation, the Alzheimer's foundation, the American Epilepsy Society and many more are doing yeoman's work in finding cures for many illnesses. To some extent, we, the people of India and other Asian countries try to follow suit, but our pace is no faster than that of a snail. In part, this is due to our ignorance about various disease processes.

For this very reason, I wish to say a few words about bone marrow transplants and how they work. I have a vision that eligible people of the Indian subcontinent ethnicity after learning a bit more about bone marrow donation, may gain some insight and understanding about the necessity of such a noble act and offer this priceless gift to those in desperate need of it.

Bone marrow is a spongy red substance present in the center of our bones including the pelvis (hips), the vertebrae (spines), the sternum (breast plate), the ribs, and the skull. This spongy red mesh contains stem cells, also known as grandfather or grandmother cells. They give rise to generations of other mature bone marrow cells which in turn create all the other present in the bloodstream, cells that deliver oxygen and other vital nutrients to different parts of the body. Normal bone marrow is like a factory, churning out as many cells as our body needs. In leukemia and other related disorders, this factory goes haywire. It produces cells that may be aggressive in competition than healthy cells, but are unable to perform their assigned functions in spite of their larger numbers. It is something like having a huge army that is totally unable to fight.

A bone marrow transplant is often the last and only treatment for curing illnesses of the blood such as Leukemia (blood cancer), lymphoma and some inherited disorders such as thalassemia major.

Transplants can be autologous or allogeneic. With autologous transplants, one receives back one's own stem cells. The stem cells first are removed and parked outside of the patient's body prior to subjecting that patient to a total-body radiation and to chemotherapy, both of which destroy the patient's bone marrow after which they are re-infused back. However, this kind of transplant is not ideal for leukemia.

With allogeneic transplants, the patient receives stem cells from the bone marrow of another person. The ideal donor is an identical twin. If this is not possible, a brother or a sister from the same parents is preferred. Unfortunately, the chance of a match from a non-identical sibling is around 25%. It implies that many patients are unable to get any match at all from their siblings. Therefore, having a donor pool becomes very important in any ethnic community, as common ethnicity increases the chances of finding a good marrow match among people who otherwise are unrelated to the patient.

The use of the word 'transplant' here might be a misnomer as in that a bone marrow transplant is not a major procedure like a kidney, heart, or liver transplant. The potential donor donates a few drops of blood to determine if his or her tissue type will match with that of the patient in question. This testing is neither terribly expensive nor difficult. Only when the tissue of a potential donor matches that of a recipient, is the donor contacted.

The main procedure of a marrow transplant or transfer requires a donor to have a few small punctures on the back of the pelvis. From these punctures, bone marrow from inside the pelvic bones (hips) is sucked out with a syringe. Such a procedure will need either general or regional (wide-area rather than local) anesthesia. As with any other surgery, some amount of post-operative soreness is often felt. This procedure only takes about one to one-and-a-half hours. Within a few weeks, the body replaces the marrow that was removed and one feels as if nothing has been taken away.

Stem cells can also be obtained from the peripheral blood. In this kind of donation process, one of the veins in the arm is used to remove the stem cells. This procedure requires the prior use of a particular medicine by the donor for four to five days in order to increase the yield of the stem cells when they are harvested. Minor temporary side effects such as bone discomfort or bone pain, muscle pain, fatigue and nausea can result from the procedure and from the medicine. Stem cells from peripheral blood are transplanted to restore diseased stem cells that have been intentionally destroyed by high-dose chemotherapy and radiation in patients suffering from the disorders mentioned above. Once the transplant is finished, the healthy cells from the donor travel to the bone marrow of the patient and begin to produce new blood cells. This restores the health of a good percentage of patients, provided no complication ensues.

Only healthy individuals between the ages of eighteen and sixty are chosen as donors for this gift of life and there is a reason for such discrimination. In donors younger than eighteen years, the issue of consent stands in the way as the procedure is considered a surgical intervention. The donor's guardian will have to be involved, both because of the law and because of ethical considerations. The limit of 60 years on the higher end is needed to make sure that the donor is relatively healthy and also to make sure that the material obtained from the donor has a good chance of survival in the recipient.

In the U.S., the National Marrow Donor Program (NMDP) provides a donor registry and communicates through a cooperative network of medical facilities present all over the country. There are similar kinds of organizations in other Western countries too. Although there are over four-and-a-half million adult volunteer donors registered in the NMDP program of the U.S., the donors from many ethnic communities, including people of the Indian subcontinent origin are difficult to find. Moreover, Asians are more polymorphic than Europeans. This means that Asians are more likely to have more than one HLA or tissue type, thus causing more difficulty in finding a compatible donor. With a larger pool of donors, the chances for locating a compatible ethnic donor becomes somewhat easier.

Through these lines of quasi-medical information, it is hoped that some members of the Indian diaspora may become motivated to help expand the donor bank and thus help the children of ethnic-Indian origin who otherwise could be waiting desperately and painfully to receive such a life-saving gift. They may not have enough time left before the flame of life simply goes dim and then extinguishes forever. By donating such a gift to a helpless child, one could simply snatch his or her life away from the jaws of death and deliver it back to the child to experience it once again in all of its glory. In my opinion, there is no better gift than saving the life of a helpless child waiting at the door of death, counting days. Such a gift not only will serve its intended purpose in saving the life of a desperate recipient but it will also bring the comfort and peace to the donor. In fact, it might well also open the doors to heaven for such a donor at the end of his or her life, especially for the one who believes in and hopes for this kind of outcome.

3.
Don't Procrastinate, Get in Shape!

The Indian immigrants of my generation, having lived in this country for quarter of a century or more, are now finally inching towards the span of their lives that many in the West refer to as the 'Golden Years'. That may be so, but a good number among the Indian diaspora do not truly see this phase of their lives as that 'Golden.'

Exploring further, one learns that significant numbers of indigenous Americans have a similar point of view. Like immigrants, the indigenous Americans also realize fully well that such a label doesn't depict a true picture of the life of the elderly and therefore a true justice is not served in calling these the 'Golden Years.'

I am a physician specializing in neurological disorders. Sitting in my office across the desk from my patients, I have the opportunity to interview a good number of people in their so-called 'Golden Years.' They often suffer from a long list of ailments usually identified with age alone; memory loss, degenerative arthritis, heart disease, stroke with paralysis, cancer and others. These poor souls often mention that there is nothing 'Golden' about these 'Golden Years' and that this label is truly ironic and perhaps uncalled for.

Immigrants from Asian countries, including India, originally came here to improve their lives, both economically and otherwise. I would not be telling the truth if I were to say differently. But in the hectic lifestyle of Western culture, many among us start ignoring one important facet of this life: the need to take care of one's physical body, the 'Temple of God.' In the process of getting rich, money-making becomes our only and ultimate goal. All else, such as family relationships, spiritual development and health takes a back seat. It is here that one ends up having problems.

Working hard, making money and getting rich, if done ethically and within the boundaries of the law, is not necessarily wrong. In a way, it is rather essential to create abundant resources to fulfill the goal of living a better lifestyle in the West. Moreover, it is the duty of each and every human being to take care of the family for this is what makes a man different from the other living creatures that happen to share this earth with us. But maintaining good personal health is an equally important issue, if not more, and cannot be entirely lost sight of.

Trapped in a cycle of day-and-night work, we first attempt to get our feet on the ground in an alien environment. As time passes and with our incessant needs and wants -- a good house, a good car, and all other sorts of paraphernalia - on a continuous upward spiral, we inadvertently turn ourselves into slaves of our ever-expanding horizon of desires. This becomes a never-ending cycle from which it becomes extremely difficult to extract ourselves without special efforts. Our weekdays are spent making money and our weekends are busy attending to family and other social gatherings, yet more necessities of this always-busy and success-driven lifestyle.

Having reached or crossed the line that arbitrarily defines the 'Golden Years,' one needs to be very cautious. One often hears about people of our ethnic background leaving this planet for the so-called heavenly abode earlier than what might have occurred otherwise. The exaggerated stress of this Western lifestyle, to which many of us were not accustomed prior to landing on these shores, coupled with a much greater intake of calorie and cholesterol-filled foods from Asian kitchens, unfortunately expedites our journey to the final destination. A total lack of organized physical exercise doesn't help either; rather, it makes this transition both rapid and real. Our habitual avoidance of medical care adds fuel to the fire by making matters even worse.

In all of this, we seem to ignore this popular saying in Hindi, "Naa rahega baanss, Na baajaigee baansury," implying that if one can't stay alive to begin with, will all of the paraphernalia to which one is so attached be of any use? It is a dilemma in which we have become trapped and seem not to have a way out. The purpose of this brief write-up is simply to reinforce what we all know and yet prefer not to know. It is essential for people approaching so-called 'middle age' to re-arrange their priorities and make the best use of whatever time they have left on this earth. We need to stop procrastinating and avoid offering silly excuses when it comes to finding time for exercise.

The healers of America, the health professionals, especially the physicians of our ethnic background, are equally at fault in putting their stamp of approval to such behaviors. Through their own examples of staying busy all the time to make few extra bucks, they end up promoting the same culture within their ethnic patients. It is a culture that emphasizes to turn the concept of making money into the mere purpose of making it and then findings ways and means, oftentimes at the fringes of law, to invest it. In this cycle, not only does one lose track of everything that is truly worth living, but it also promotes the concept of keeping busy to make money at the expense of maintaining health and healthy lifestyle. As has been mentioned in this Biblical saying, "Physician, heal thyself," it is all too true, as doctors - indigenous as well as immigrant - are just as guilty of ignoring as anyone else focusing on dollars and neglecting their own health.

It goes without saying that even in the busiest of the schedules one can always find creative means to take care of oneself and stay fit; all that is needed is the motivation. Taking proper care of oneself does not necessarily require any special efforts. Regular exercise can be made a part of one's schedule in our daily lives. A walk in the neighborhood, as many of us often used to take back home, is something nearly everyone can do. Yogic exercises, using a treadmill at home, or working out in a structured environment like a gym, all happen to be good options. I vividly remember those walks around the host's house after weekend dinner parties, back when our community was small and those gatherings were cozy. Instead of fulfilling the definition of 'couch potato' by sitting on a sofa and watching TV, we often took the opportunity to enjoy a walk for a mile or two.

During working hours, the stairs can easily be used for getting to different floors rather than using elevators, especially in multi-story office buildings. Brisk walks in the corridors of large office building is another easy way to get the needed exercise. Weather permitting, one could go to lunch on foot rather than driving. Parking the car at a distance from the entrance of one's office or work place rather than closer is a smart way to get some exercise that costs nothing. While sitting and watching TV, isometric exercises can be easily performed. Strolling through the corridors of climate-controlled shopping malls is a very creative as well as entertaining way of getting needed exercise without much hassle. In fact, options in the Western countries are plentiful. The missing link is the lack of motivation or a will to get in shape.

It should not be forgotten, however, that spending each day in procrastination, only takes us closer to our final destination. We all know fully well that one day the final act of this life's drama has to be played out. But while the show is on, there is nothing wrong in making it more pleasant and healthier. In order to do so, we must make real efforts to get into shape and leave procrastination behind, allowing this final act of mortal life to be played out well and enjoyed happily.

.

.

4.
Grass Always Looks Greener in the 'Phorren-Lands'!

Every so often we hear stories about young Indians, especially Punjabis, leaving their homes in a quest to find their dream destinations in the West. In order to help fulfill their dreams, the families of these young men dole out a good chunk of their paltry possessions. Many of them end up mortgaging their properties after they have sold their liquid assets. Some even end up selling whatever small piece of agricultural land they own in order to arrange for the fare and the exorbitant fees demanded by unscrupulous travel agents and middlemen. The process sometimes leads to financial ruin for the families.

Still, parents reluctantly make such precarious decisions in the hopes that their children might make good in that hitherto-unknown fairyland about which they have heard much but seen nothing. In deep corners of their hearts, the parents carry a lingering hope that once their children establish themselves, they will chip in and take care of their aging parents. But, alas! It is wishful thinking, at best.

Unfortunately for some of these young men, their journeys to the fantasy-lands are cut short en route through unnatural and painful deaths. Tragic stories often appear in the world press detailing the horrendous amounts of hardships and torture that some of these individuals often endure in trying to fulfill their dreams. Travel agents are usually blamed and rightly so for many of the woes of these young and immature travelers. More often than not, it is the travel agents who entrap these unsuspecting young men for the imaginary greener pastures in foreign lands. But the story doesn't end here. There are several other elements that ultimately force young Indians, mostly rural Punjabis, to take such a dangerous plunge.

Ongoing economic problems in Punjab are mostly the consequences of poor governance for several years both at the central and the state levels. The long-standing feudal conflicts between the powerful rural-based Sikh *Akali* leadership in combination with city-based Hindu *BJP* on one hand, and the Congress Party on the other, keep busy in settling scores against one another in a never-ending battle. At the same time the financial conditions of ordinary people is continuously going down the drain. Economic regression has been taking its toll, emptying the coffers of people as well as of the government for long. On top of it all, the job situation for the young and rural populace of India on the whole, and the state of Punjab in particular, has been depressed for quite some time. Lack of creative planning has dampened an already negligible job market.

The education system in India, especially in the Punjab, is so antiquated that it completely fails to recognize the changing circumstances. The needs of the present world economies are altogether different than what they had been in the past. There are several engineering schools in the Punjab, but the absence of heavy industry precludes the trained newcomers from finding suitable jobs within the state itself. Appropriate emphasis is not placed on training these young men in modern-day trades needed for day-to-day jobs.

The failure of the Indian psyche and culture to provide dignity and respect for the manual trades and crafts prevents youth from directing their energy toward technical schools. Moreover an obvious lack of love for labor and for the 'blue collar jobs' makes such work unattractive for the so-called educated class, even if it were made available. Rather, these semi-educated young men keep on day-dreaming about an unseen 'glitzy' life abroad while constantly whining about what they don't and do have.

As a consequence, one finds an abundance of unemployed young men having advanced degrees in subjects for which there are no markets. A few lucky ones might be able to find some scarce teaching jobs in their subjects but even those fields are already full to the brim and there are far fewer openings than needed to accommodate huge armies of such available candidates. Hordes of unemployed young boys and girls, fully 'suited and booted' in well-ironed dresses, having nothing else to do, are often seen strolling in city bazaars, trying to attract young men or women of opposite sex. They are totally oblivious to the amount of hard work put in by their counterparts in the Western world who had to regularly sweat in kitchens of the restaurants washing dishes, or stacking boxes in warehouses of grocery stories, just to collect a few dollars (or Euros) to support themselves.

On top of it, with every subsequent generation, India's population keeps on growing exponentially, thanks to our theoretical emphasis on the family planning that may appear good on paper but has no true effect on the rising population. The rapidly-expanding numbers of eligible landholders cannot be supported by the diminishing reserves of agricultural land that they inherit from their parents.

In the past, one fourth of the Indian defense force consisted of Sikh soldiers primarily from rural backgrounds of Punjab. The martial qualities of the Sikh people, especially the rural class, made the British rulers of India to preferentially seek their entry into various branches of the military, air force and navy. Their entry into armed services acted as a safety valve providing an outlet for young Punjabi farmers who otherwise would have become landless and jobless. It helped to ease the burden of dependence upon a limited amount of available agricultural land. However, since partition and after India got its freedom, the attention given to this segment of society for their unquestioned martial abilities unfortunately has been slowly and steady withdrawn, thanks to a changed and somewhat unfavorable political environment in this aspect. The situation was further exacerbated by the political upheavals of Punjab in the 1980s.

During the latter part of this past century, Western countries, especially Canada and the U.K., maintained an open-door policy toward immigration from former British colonies in Asia and elsewhere. This proved greatly helpful in reducing the numbers of unemployed youths in those countries. The eagerness to leave homes for exploring 'phorren lands' is partly fueled by the glitzy images of the West included in thousands of the Indian movies churned out every year by Bollywood and regularly shown in the movie theaters across India. The superficial affluence exhibited by visiting non-resident Indian (NRI) to his native village adds fuel to the fire. Shining gold-plated wristwatches, big gold necklaces, fancy electronic gadgets and other paraphernalia brought back to his hometown by an NRI from 'phorren' sojourn attracts unemployed youths like bees to honey.

It doesn't take long for impressionable youths to become mesmerized by the superficialities of the Western lifestyle as presented through the distorted prism of such a visitor to his home village.

Mesmerized by such an image of the West, the moment arrives when unemployed young men take the ultimate plunge. Going through dangerous journeys across oceans, through many continents and countries, they eventually arrive in 'the lands' of their dreams, assuming they survive the journeys. But alas! As soon as they touch the shores of their destinations, their dreams get shattered. They soon find out that the fantasy-lands they had been looking for, are nowhere to be found unless one is qualified enough and is able to communicate effectively in the local language. With no work in sight and no money in their pockets, they are good for nothing.

This creates a ripe environment for these young men to walk a path that is less than desirable than they had intended. Instead of finding the heaven of their long-awaited dreams, they end up working in small kitchens of Desi-owned or operated restaurants, gas stations or corner stores. Working for twelve to eighteen hours a day, seven days a week, every day of the year, without any vacations, they still cannot save enough to do what they had hoped. Any spare change that they managed to save is wiped out through endless trips to the offices of lawyers for the next ten to fifteen years or even more in the hopes of finding ways to settle permanently in the countries of the West.

Had these menial jobs not come their way through the benevolence of their own people in business, many young immigrants would not have been able to hold their feet on the ground of their dream fantasy-lands. A visit back home to their parents becomes next to impossible, not only because they have no money, but also because of the labyrinth of rules and regulations for re-entry into their host countries. One by one, their aging parents leave this world, taking with them their desire to see the face of their 'Pardesi' child or grandchild. Those who left their newlywed wives behind painfully find out on return that age has caught up with their spouses. Their hair is turned grey from spending endless and sleepless dark nights alone while their children have turned into adults and become distant.

The mental state of such a young man can be compared to that of a snake having a lizard in its teeth that could neither be eaten nor left. The green grass of the 'distant lands' turns yellow, slowly but surely, right in front of his eyes. However, the illusory attraction of these 'fantasy-lands' in minds of the future upcoming Generations Y and Z, born of Generation X in India, never dies down. Rather, it keeps on thriving as passionately as it always was in the previous Generation X. This illusion of hope keeps them in a permanent wait for the appearance of that rare silver-lining someday, somewhere. Only a few lucky ones, if this is what being 'lucky' is, may find their dreams finally come true. Yet the price one pays for such dreams may or may not be worth it , depending upon how one looks at this kind of life, even if it were to be called a life at all.

5.
Old Habits Never Die

A few centuries ago Waaris Shah, a highly-celebrated Punjabi poet, penned a masterpiece epic about a traditional Punjabi love story called *'Heer Raanjha.'* In his poem, two famous couplets are mentioned that go something like this, *"Vaadriaan sjaadriaan nibhen siraan de naal."* and *"Waaris Shah naa aadtaan jandhiaan jee, Bhanvain katiaye porian porian jee."* What he implied through these lines was, "Old habits will stay put with a person all the way through to the end." And "Even if one is cut, limb by limb or finger by finger, the habits will never disappear, so sayeth Waaris Shah."

True to this statement we, the people of India, still keep on clinging to some of our old habits, even if they have become totally outdated, outmoded for the rest of the world and appear purposeless. No attempt is ever made to put such habits to a permanent rest, despite the fact that they might have been completely abandoned in the remainder of the world and for good reasons. Interestingly, the practitioners of such traditions, even if they are fully aware of the negatives, will not discard them altogether. They are always ready to provide a detailed account of what is bad about those habits, yet in the next breath, they can justify equally well in retaining them .

My point is easily clarified by looking at any situation that requires us to form a 'disciplined queue.' Whenever there is more than one individual, the result is usually mayhem. We have all witnessed incidents where our people -- without any regard to the number of persons standing in an established queue - try to jump ahead to be first in the line. Such behaviors can be seen many times and at many places, be it for the purchase of a ticket for the movie or for a bus ride, or for any other purpose. People believe that without showing this hurried type of aggressiveness, they might miss the boat. On the other hand, we all have observed that even the poor little ants, representing one of the lowest forms of life on this earth, usually tend to follow each other in queues while trying to collect food and materials for their very survival.

Ironically, even after having been exposed to the Western culture for long time, our people on returning home either tend to forget or intentionally ignore the norms of behavior that they observed and to some extent practiced abroad. They suddenly revert back to their old habits and mimic the behavior of the local crowd around them.

I am reminded of one incident that I witnessed at the New Delhi airport while I was returning to the United States after a short term visit to India. Most of the passengers on that flight were of Indian origin but had made their homes in the West. A bus was arranged by the airline to take us back to a hotel for an overnight stay as our flight had been cancelled. Now, it was fairly obvious that all the passengers will have to be accommodated and that the bus could only leave once everyone was on board. The bus driver asked the passengers to form a queue for entry onto the bus. One of the passengers in front of the queue had some physical weakness in his legs and was unable to board the bus as easily and quickly as others. All of the passengers behind him kept on gradually moving in front, pushing him aside while ignoring his disability. The disabled passenger ended up at the end of the queue through no fault of his own.

In the same queue were two Westerners who were watching what was going on. The behavior of the passengers truly bothered them, and finally one of them collected some courage and said, "Look gentlemen! All of us are going to the same hotel and this bus is not going to leave until everybody is taken care of. Why on earth is there a need for us to shove this helpless person around? Why can't we let this man take his turn? He is not even asking to be ahead of anybody."

But what the foreigner said fell on deaf ears. It was here that I realized that what Waaris had said many centuries ago in those couplets was exactly on the mark and right. Living abroad might make one clever and rich in certain ways, but the habits learned in the childhood and youth -- especially the bad ones -- will stay put, no matter what.

The most common thing about 'common sense' is that it is not that common. In the above scenario, common sense dictated that if there was a bus meant for a specific group of people to be taken to one common destination in one trip, it did not matter then as to who got on the bus first, second or at the end. Someone might respond that the time one boards the bus determines what seat one gets. But how much difference would it truly have made by occupying a seat in the back of the bus instead of the front, when the entire trip was not going to take more than a few minutes?

Another phenomenon that I would like to comment upon is the way we run our meetings as opposed to how meetings are run by Westerners. Many of us with experiences

51

in different types of group meetings should not have any difficulty in realizing what I am about to say.

Compared to Westerners, we have a hard time containing our thoughts about the issue under discussion. We try to interject, object or otherwise intervene and cut short the person who is speaking. There is no consideration of taking turns and there is no decorum. Interrupting others and losing our cool by raising our voices is what we do best. Invariably, we are convinced of our righteousness, even if the point under discussion might not be in agreement with our view. We think we know better, and therefore, we must be listened to first. A sense of discipline or the patience to listen to other's point of view seems to take a back seat. Understandably, part of the problem might be related to language barriers. By no means do I imply that the indigenous population is free of such deficiencies. They too have issues that are equally, if not more, annoying.

We live in a country where the language of the majority is English. Oftentimes, we start conversing among one another in our own language and simply ignore the fact that the others around us might not understand our language. In doing so, we pay little or no regard to their feelings. Imagine ourselves in a group where the majority doesn't understand our language. Would we not feel ignored, secluded, or slighted when the group starts conversing in a language that is foreign to us? Isn't it likely that others might have similar feelings when we converse loudly in our language, a language that they don't understand? One could say that everybody has a right to his or her style. But then at the same time, it shouldn't be forgotten that such a right doesn't provide anyone any authority to insist that others have to modify and follow our style?

My purpose here is simply to point out the differences that I see in our attitudes and behaviors as opposed to the established norms of the country in which we have decided to settle. The first step in modifying a behavior will be to become aware of its effects upon other people. That awareness makes it much easier to tackle such differences later on. I fully understand that what I have said here might not be applicable to many people of my culture and as such it might not fit their mold. And for those of you who already have shed this unfortunate cultural baggage, my congratulations.

SQUARE PEGS, ROUND HOLES

6.
The Concept of Family:
Here and There

The year was 1972 and the place was Booth Memorial Medical Center, a private community hospital in Flushing, Queens, that was then a beautiful suburb of New York City. I began my journey from my hometown of Patiala in the state of Punjab, India. After having been through a tedious process of completing formalities for foreign travel that required running from office to office in New Delhi and spending my last penny in fighting red tape, I finally boarded a plane from India's capital. I landed at JFK International Airport in New York in the late evening. A taxi hired by Booth Memorial Medical Center, my employer, picked me up and dropped me in front of the hospital.

The next day morning, I was ushered into the human resources department of the hospital to sign documents to begin my internship in the department of medicine. As it was my first working day in this country, everything was new and there was a lot to learn. While filling out the application, I encountered one of the most important cultural differences between people from the East and those of my host country. It made me realize right there and then that the way we look at life and accept our relationships with our near and dear ones is different from those of the people among whom I have chosen to live.

Going over the application, the individual assigned to assist me in filling it out, asked about the kind of health coverage I would need. I happened to respond that I would like to include my family in this plan. She got somewhat perplexed for I had just stated earlier that I wasn't married and therefore, did not have a wife or children, so why should I even be bothering to ask for their insurance? Little did I realize that the concept of the word 'family' in my mind was entirely different from that of the prevalent culture of the West? In the Indian context, parents and siblings also happen to be part of the immediate family, which is not the case here. Finding me baffled, she tried to comfort me by adding that such relations do not constitute the 'core family' in this culture and they are often labeled as 'folks.'

The same dynamics are relevant when we dissect and analyze the genesis of certain words in the English language pertaining to family relations. English is the most commonly-spoken language in the West, yet it doesn't seem to have specific words for many family relationships. A language always relates to a group of people and its culture and its vocabulary draws from that. Therefore, it is just natural that family relations considered unimportant in the Western culture, will not have suitable words in its language. For example, the Westerners attach 'in-law(s)' at the end of a relationship to make it work for an equivalent relationship which they inherit from their spouses simply because relationship of the spouse does not carry too much significance for an individual in the Western culture. The mother of one's spouse, known as *'Saus'* in Indian vernacular becomes mother-in-law, while the father of spouse, the Indian *'Sasur or Saura,'* is known as father-in–law.

Additionally, the culture here doesn't object to addressing the father-in-law or the mother-in-law by his or her first name. This again is something unheard of in Eastern cultures. By calling such relations by their first names and not addressing them as moms or dads, reduces the feeling of intimacy that they otherwise deserve. That is why the daughters-in-law of Western culture, most of the time, don't have much to do with their in-laws and often lump them together as 'our folks.' Likewise, the attitudes of sons-in-law mirror those of the daughters-in-law. All in all, the relationships seem to be limited to the parents or maybe to the grandparents within the culture of the West.

Furthermore, *'Bhatteejaa'* or *'Bhaanjaa'* and *'Bhatteejee'* or *'Bhaanjee'* are all recognized under one simple relation of nephew and niece instead of having specific equivalent words for each as is the case in Indian languages. Similarly *'Chaachaa'* or *'Maama'* and *'Chaachi'* or *'Maami'*, specific words in Eastern languages meant for specific relations, could only be distinguished in the English language by using adjectives like paternal uncle or maternal uncle, or wife of paternal uncle or wife of maternal uncle. One has to depend upon additional clarification for the relationship of *'Jeeja Ji'* as opposed to *'Saala Sahib'* by explaining it further as the husband of one's sister or the brother of one's wife. The sister of the wife, the sister of the husband, and for that matter the wife of the brother, are all lumped together under a single term of sister-in-law, in the English language instead of *'Saali Sahiba'*, *'Nanand'*, or *'Bhuji'*, *'Bhabhi'*, etc., and thus the list goes on.

Isn't it ironic that the most common language of the world, English, fails us when it comes to explaining the deepest and most personal relationships of the family? The language of the West seems to give us a hint that such family relations do not mean much in the Western culture. The paucity of such words in the language of the West could be simply considered an outward manifestation of how a Western mind accepts these relationships.

On the other hand, now look at the names of the body parts. Fingers and toes are identified separately and with distinct words in English. That is in stark contrast to Indian languages where they are all known as fingers of the hands or fingers of the feet. One could simply interpret this as indicating that the Eastern culture cares little when it comes to self-recognition or self-importance. Putting it in another way, one can say that English, the language of the West, seems to care more towards self, perhaps mirroring the underlying selfish thought processes of some of the people to whom it belongs.

Moving further along, one notices that it is the same attitude that makes children of West book seats for their elderly parents in nursing homes without any remorse whatsoever, at least equal to what the people of East would have shown under such situations. Perhaps the necessities of Western life make it imperative for both husband and wife to find jobs in order to have a reasonable living, leaving little time for the kind of care that their parents need in home settings. But notwithstanding such realities, these are not the only motives for pushing elderly parents out. It is the remoteness of inner connections and the coldness of un-cemented relationships from early childhood that ultimately leads to such painful decisions.

The parents in such situations are not entirely blameless

for they also played negative roles by actively encouraging separation during their heydays. In our homelands of the past, did we ever come across Adult Residential Localities, the likes of which we have here? I'm referring to places like Sun City, Arizona, where the minimum age for a resident is fixed at fifty-five. These senior residents usually don't welcome younger individuals to live in places specifically designated for them for they think that the younger residents could upset the peace and tranquility of their more sedentary lifestyle that they happen to crave for. What a strange logic!

Another important aspect of the Western culture that erodes the very roots of the Eastern concept of family, relates to the way children are asked to vacate their parent's home upon their entry into the adulthood. Talk to any parent here, and the feeling will be that once a child turns eighteen, he or she becomes a burden. The richest of the rich parents expects the children to pay for their own education as well as for their marriages; some will even ask for rent if a child lives at home while attending college. The culture expects them to work and earn their own way once they have come of age. The logic given here is that this is the only way growing children will learn to become independent. Obviously one cannot and should not deny that self-reliance is definitely imperative after a certain age. The sooner a child embarks on a program of self-reliance, the earlier he or she will become self-sufficient yet self-sufficiency should not bring in a feeling of burden at any cost under any circumstance.

In some situations, it is the children who decide on their own to leave the nest as soon as they turn eighteen. But the consequences of such a major step initiated either by parents or children when the teenager is still an immature adult, often cuts the very roots of a growing plant that is yet to flourish on its own. This attitude of parents towards their children may leave its adverse imprints upon their tender minds, causing a heavy toll later on in the relationship between parents and children. The increasing fragility of this connection can break the ultimate parent-child bond. By then, there is little point for the parents to 'cry over spilled milk' and regret the distance they put between themselves and their children.

The most important difference in the practice of these two cultures relates to how we understand and practice the concept of family. One needs to keep in mind that 'family' is the foundation upon which the rest of human relationships develop and thrive. Therefore, acknowledgement and respect for strong family concepts early on will ultimately support a durable and long lasting family structure.

7.

The Practice of Safety is Often Alien to the Indian Culture

The practice of safety in the Western culture is consciously highlighted and clearly understood from early childhood. On the other hand, those of us who had the opportunity to live in India before permanently migrating to the West will be in a relatively better position to clearly understand the almost 'non-existent' concept of safety in relation to the culture back home. Our concerns most of the time, were primarily directed to the fulfillment of day-to-day needs. In order to achieve these objectives, we often gravitated towards short-term gains irrespective of what ensued en route. Safety for self or for the other people was not felt to be a big consideration. There never was any type of training or special education in schools or colleges or, for that matter, in the work environments about the concept of safety. No doubt, the situation over time has changed to some extent more or less.

In Eastern culture, there is no defined method of accepting the responsibility or assigning it to someone else for the consequences of an action gone awry. In fact to a certain extent, the term 'responsibility' for paying back to the aggrieved party in the form of a formal compensation for a wrongful act has been missing from our dictionary, at least in the past. Legal battles are arduous, ineffective and impossible to afford for an ordinary aggrieved individual. The mighty ones among the society always find ways to avoid penalties using their political muscle and connections, especially if the injured individual happens to be poor and unable to stand up to the challenge.

Most of the time, the agenda of the politicians as well as of the bureaucrats of India, is primarily limited to the methods of how far and how rapidly they can skim the country and their countrymen. The accumulation of personal wealth by hook or crook and to the extent possible, within the shortest time span, the time they might hold the office, remains the only goal in their minds. The concern for the safety and well-being of their constituents is not their collective cups of tea for it is not where they think their pockets are.

Having said so, it is important to realize that lack of safety in day-to-day life in India is not a consequence of simple negligence. There are too many other complex issues. Some are simply incorrigible and beyond control. A simple discussion here, it is hoped, might turn out to be a catalyst in reinforcing the urgency of its awareness.

Like elsewhere in the world, each and every person in India loves to drive a vehicle. But the similarity ends here. One of the most painful issues that need perusal relates to the mere numbers of roadside accidents every day on the highways and byways of India. This drama in relation to the loss of life unfolds relentlessly on the streets of India everywhere. Our nihilistic attitude as a consequence of our failure to find justice from the law enforcement agencies coupled with complacency at the top ranks ends up inducing and then maintaining this painful and unacceptable status quo.

Most of us are aware of large number of seriously maimed persons as a result of avoidable accidents. The safety laws meant to protect the passengers or the drivers of the motor vehicles are easily floundered by all simply because the human life is viewed far too cheaply in India. To reinforce my point, I am including the following incident:-

During one of my visits to India, I hired a taxi-cab. Unfortunately the seat belt of this cab on the passenger side was broken. As soon as I occupied the front seat, the driver handed me a thin black rope, less than one centimeter in diameter, hanging from the passenger side door of the taxi. He asked me to tuck it into the belt of my pants. On questioning, "What use will this thin rope be in case of an accident?" his response was not only amusing but scary. He informed me that since the original seat belt was broken, he was using this black rope in its place to avoid getting a traffic ticket en route.

After further discussion about protection, he stated, "The issue is not protection, sir. What is important here is that I should have something that looks like a belt, working or not, strong or weak, so that the policeman will have some excuse to let me go after taking care of his pocket and not pursue the matter further. And this string looks like a belt. Doesn't it sir?" I certainly was left speechless and helpless. It was a true eye opener for me. From his response, it was obvious that the governmental agencies were totally oblivious and hardly concerned about the real purpose of buckling up. It was more like a ritual for the drivers and a way for the policemen to skim some extra bucks through the harassment of the public.

Driving in India is not the only hazard. The tragedies from electrocutions are fairly rampant in India, especially in monsoon months. Paying a little heed to the common sense could easily prevent their occurances. Partially damaged, totally rusted and shabbily bent electric poles with heavy wires hanging loose, close to the rooftops of residences and businesses offer an open invitation to electrocutions. They become an easy source for fire hazards that, in turn, cause many unfortunate accidents. A lack of awareness about safety in the minds of consumers and negligence on the part of the utility departments often leads to these horrific but avoidable tragedies. With employees having little or no training in this regard, what else could one expect? The poor linemen, at the bottom of the totem pole and without any understanding of the danger, will always be asked to climb the electric poles to repair those live wires without any protective gear or safety tools. The availability of such tools and gear is entirely dependent upon the rank of the worker simply because the value of life isn't gauged the same for different ranks.

The list of incidences of loss of human lives in every facet of living is too long and too well-known. If things go wrong, our ingrained beliefs in pre-ordained destiny lead us to believe that these acts were simply the 'Will of God.' Yet avoiding injuries from preventable accidents by paying due attention to safety, if not for ourselves, at least for our families should have been our prime concern instead.

One sincerely hopes that the people of India, long affected adversely either through their own negligence or that of the others, will finally wake up one day and try to take their destinies into their own hands. With the world becoming smaller and the cultural finesse of the West infiltrating all over, even in the remotest places of India, the long awaited awareness about safety among our people should not lag far behind. By trying to learn the strict rules of safety practice, both in spirit and in action from our Western partners on this earth and accepting responsibilities for our unsafe behaviors could certainly benefit our people. A safety-conscious culture and society can always make life easier for all. Instead of becoming mere statistics of injury and death due to a simple lack of awareness about safety, it is much better to pay heed to its simple rules and avoid an unfortunate outcome. This might allow one to enjoy the mortal life a bit more on this mother earth.

8.

To Shake Hands or To Fold Hands?

We, the people of Indian subcontinent, irrespective of our faiths and places of residence, have a feeling of uneasiness in our minds in carrying out Eastern traditions in our adopted foreign culture. The basic concepts behind many of our Eastern traditions are not that clear and oftentimes may not be known to us; hence our ignorance leads to a kind of hesitancy within us. Sometimes even if we happen to be aware of their significance, we may yet fail to explain the importance to others. Be that as it may, our lack of awareness about the origin and background of Eastern traditions certainly doesn't mean that such customs are superfluous and need to be discarded. On the other hand, every custom or tradition with an intrinsic Western origin or value appears superior to us. Without fully understanding their basis, a simple label of a custom being Western in origin finds a preferable spot within us. But the implications of following customs and traditions without knowing their intrinsic rationales may sometimes turn out to be less than satisfactory.

In our failure to understand the basis for some of our own traditions, we often resort to offering pseudo-explanations that do not appeal to inquisitive minds. Just because our elders did something this way or that way is not a sufficient or convincing explanation in the modern Western world. The modern mind, having been exposed to significant Western influences, takes nothing for granted and oftentimes refuses to accept Eastern concepts at their face value. It seeks to measure everything with a scientific yardstick, most of the time.

Unfortunately, we often do not pay serious heed to the thousands of years of indigenous wisdom imparted to us by our ancestors as well as by seers and sages of India. By not applying their concepts within the parameters of modern science, not only do we fail ourselves in the process but we fail them too. When we try to understand our age-old customs in the light of modern science, it becomes obvious that our ancestors had definitely done their homework, albeit in their own ways. Understanding this fundamental fact will certainly help forestall the rush to accept certain untenable customs of the West. At the same time, some age-old customs of the East that have withstood the test of time will be spared from being casually mutilated.

It is with these thoughts in mind that I wish to draw attention to the proven advantages of the age-old Indian custom of wishing one another well without touching hands. We somehow feel ashamed in practicing this indigenous Indian style, openly and freely, especially after we decide to live in the West. We believe that by not acting like others and refusing to shake hands in this society gives the impression that we are behind time and somewhat less polite than others. Instead shaking hands in accordance with the prevalent

Western tradition, while keeping our age-old tradition of folding hands on the back burner imparts a feeling of our 'being and becoming modern'.

Little do we realize however, that the Indian custom of greeting one another does have a proven medical advantage over the Western style of handshake? A greeting of '*Namaste,*' '*Sat Sri Akaal,*' more appropriately '*Waheguru Ji Ka Khalsa, Waheguru Ji Ki Fateh,*' and '*Assalamu Alaikum,*' whatever the case might be, doesn't include hand touching. Rather, in these Eastern customs, the hands are not put forward to make physical contact with the hands of the person being greeted. Both individuals in a greeting mode simply fold their hands or gesture in a set pattern of wishing one another well. '*Namaste*' and '*Sat Sri Akaal*' have their origin in India and are used as a greeting at the time of welcoming or saying good-bye to another individual like hello or good-bye here in the West.

According to Wikipedia (the Internet encyclopedia), the word '*Namas*' in '*Namaste*' stands for 'bow, obeisance, reverential salutation or adoration, and the word '*te*' is the grammatical form of the personal pronoun '*tvam*' or you. Put together, the literal translation of '*Namaste*' turns out to be reverential salutation to you. '*Sat Sri Akaal*' is commonly used by Sikhs and literally means 'God is Truth' or 'Truth is God.' Historically well-informed and religiously-oriented Sikhs will often use the salutation of '*Waheguru Ji Ka Khalsa, Waheguru Ji Ki Fateh.*' It translates into 'Hail the pure ones who belong to the Lord God, Hail the Lord God, to whom belongs the victory.' '*Assalamu Alaikum*' is the Muslim way of greeting that means, 'Peace be upon you.'

Again as per Wikipedia, greeting others by bowing, in which the head or the entire upper body is lowered, is primarily practiced by the people of the Orient, especially the Japanese. Some accompanying soft words may also be spoken. However, the bottom line is that no Eastern custom involves touching another person's hands; there is no bodily contact during greeting.

By contrast, in Western cultures one puts one's hand forward for the other to touch or shake during the process of salutation. The writer, Peter Urs Bender mentions in Canada-One magazine that hand shaking is a cultural behavior or a custom made popular by English people. Putting the hand forward was done to show to the other that one is open-handed and doesn't have a weapon hidden in one's hand. What needs to be realized here is that this custom has nothing to do with the character of a person, for it is not an inborn behavior; rather it is a learned one, a cultural artifact from a time long past. This fact is stated by many other writers, including Dr. Desmond Morris and Sami Molcho in their writings on body language. On the other hand, many seem to consider that a physical touch with the person who is being greeted makes for a closer relationship and shaking of the hands signals the warmth as well as strength of the person who is greeting. This may be true to some extent, but it is becoming more and more obvious that such a close contact has its own medical perils and therefore, might well be both unnecessary and unwise.

Jeremy Stone, replying in an Internet response about the topic of SARS and handshaking in the Yale Global Forum, stated, "Hand-shaking is a form of human contact that is unnecessary and, from an epidemic point of view, unfortunate." The medical community has long emphasized the significance of frequent hand-washing in the prevention of infections. Unfortunately, in practice, even people in the medical field seem to pay no more than lip-service to healthy practices when it comes to greetings. We repeatedly touch our eyes and our noses without thinking, and if one happens to be infected with a virus, that virus can be transmitted to any individual with whom the hands are shaken.

Dr. Julie Gerberding, the director of Centers for Disease Control in Atlanta once noted: "Nothing is more effective than the habitual use of hand-washing. Yet not more than two-thirds of the people wash their hands even after going to the washroom." Now, if this is true -- and I have no doubt that it is -- would it not imply that the less we touch each other's hands, the better it will be for all of us? But watch the resistance in changing this behavior. History tells us and experience confirms that human nature accepts new information with difficulty. It is well-known to all of us that the world is round, and it was round long before this fact became known. Yet there was a great amount of resistance in accepting this fact when all what people could see of the world appeared flat to them. Many forces tried their best to uphold the idea of a 'Flat Earth' and they vehemently opposed anyone who claimed or tried to prove otherwise.

The age-old Eastern tradition of greeting one another without imposing the use of hands turns out to be on the right side of modern science. For once, Eastern philosophy and behavior seems to be far ahead of modern prevalent Western styles and thus should act as a wake-up call for all those who tend to denigrate every Eastern custom. There doesn't seem to be any valid scientific reason to simply discard the hygienically-correct Eastern styles of salutations such as '*Namaste*,' '*Sat Sri Akaal*,' or '*Aassalamu Aiekum*,' even while living in the Western environments. Rather, each one of the diaspora members should be actively working as an ambassador in not only practicing it within their own community but also sincerely trying to disseminate the usefulness of our age-old proven styles of salutations to the public of the West at-large.

SQUARE PEGS, ROUND HOLES

9.

The Most Painful Times
for Diaspora Members

With appropriate modifications of its environment, a plant can survive and grow in an unnatural habitat, though its robustness, the juices within its fruits and the beauty of its flowers will always fall short of its expected potential. An analysis of the mental framework of members of the diaspora by an astute observer will expose a similar phenomenon.

Many immigrants have created wonders for themselves in these wonderlands and their stories are all too well-known. But while they happen to be living physically abroad, something always seems to be amiss in their minds. In spite of all of their successes and the many advantages of living in affluent nations, they always yearn for the lands of their birth as well as for the closeness of their relatives and friends, whether they may acknowledge it openly or not.

Subconscious elements of anguish become uncovered when one receives tragic news of the sudden demise of a near relative or a dear friend back home. Such painful moments in the lives of diaspora members hurt them deeply regardless of how long they have lived away from their native cultures and places as well as how successful they have been in their materialistic lives abroad. Deep anguish begins to replace the superficial happiness on their faces. Their fresh outlooks get replaced with sunken-eyed sullenness. The true psychic impact of long distance and desolate loneliness of an affected immigrant becomes obvious at such times only. Faced with such a dilemma, an affected individual wishes to fly away back home like a bird, to be with those from whom one had been plucked.

"Alas! I wish I could have been there with rest of my family at this time to share their pains!" Such statements of despair and longing are commonly heard when close connections of blood and friendship are severed by death, all the more so when 'home' is an alien land far from one's grieving family and friends. However, despite chronic suppressed urges and desires, it is often too late to reclaim those moments, for the train had already left the station.

The prolonged lack of physical contact with near and dear ones, and the guilt of having been far removed from the deceased prior to his or her passing away, often generates a feeling of anguish and self-deprecation within an expatriate's mind. One often starts wondering about the precious lost moments that were meant to be spent in the company of those back home, but which were purposefully treaded upon for greener pastures. Time lost does not return. Putting on a strong face at such times is just a mere attempt to appear strong in the eyes of friends and family, for it is human nature not to show weakness.

It is here that one starts to re-think life's priorities. Despite the easy availability of all the material comforts and pleasures for which one had left one's native land, the joy of such life seems to lose its meaning. The helplessness of the situation and the superficiality of one's new existence begin to take on a different meaning. The attachment with the country of one's birth and deeper connections with blood relatives and old friends start appearing once again on the life-screen up-front. One begins to take stock of the true loss that has been sustained with a move to the newer world. The words of the English poet Sir Walter Scott, "Those who decide to leave their motherland, in fact, die a doubly death" written in the poem 'My Native Land' starts making all the sense once again.

In the same breath, it needs to be said; however, that in this day and age one could simply not afford to stay glued to the home country forever. The times and necessities of life have changed, and one's attachments must change as well. The world is truly shrinking and life is changing at a faster pace. Breaking away from one's roots is a natural process in the evolution of all living creatures, regardless of where they happen to reside. Psychological and physical interdependence upon relatives and friends is getting remoter and remoter simply because fissures are developing faster and turning deeper. And those who wish to live closer with family and friends may not be able to do so any more for one or the other reason, even in India.

The immigrants who left India or Indian subcontinent in the 1960s and 1970s will never forget those times when even a phone call back home took hours or days, especially if the loved ones lived outside in smaller towns or rural areas. I vividly remember the time, some thirty plus years ago, when our first son was born. I wanted to share my excitement right away with my parents in India. But the telephone exchange system took over three days before I could even get connected. In fact, a telegram made its way through much earlier and faster than the telephone.

And yet, the times have clearly changed, and changed for the better. International travel has become easy and fast. For many, the fear of being unreachable is considered obsolete. One can physically reach almost any corner of the globe within twenty-four hours if the need arises, though of course, with minors expected difficulties inherent in international travel. Moreover with the passage of time, some of the members of the diaspora now have the company of their close relatives and friends right here in these countries, allowing one to make needed arrangements with a cool mind at such times.

Now let us consider the other side. No one ever forced us to leave our own countries in order to settle in far-away lands. Rather, many of us have migrated abroad on our own sweet choice. In fact, even now, given the opportunity, the entire population of the Third World would wish to migrate to the so-called advanced Western nations. Yet as we have seen, even the most advantageous moves, away from the mother countries to the far-away lands will bring with them their own set of problems to a greater or lesser extent.

It is important here to remind ourselves that death must come to all, regardless of where one lives. We all must leave this earth once we have done our time. Death will not pause merely because it will be inconvenient or painful for the members of the diaspora as they happen to be far removed from their loved ones. One may win one way yet is likely to lose the other way; having it both ways falls within the domain of only a very few lucky ones. And finally it might not be out of place here to recall that oft-repeated statement, *"Every rose has a thorn."* What a truth!

10.
The Expression of Spousal Love Stays Intact Despite Losing Marbles

As part of my professional work, I come across elderly patients with disorders of intellectual decline. In the usual medical jargon, these individuals are grouped under the heading of what is commonly known as 'Alzheimer's disease.' In fact having spent close to 35 years in the specialty of neurology, under whose auspicious this illness usually falls, I have seen hundreds and hundreds of such patients, if not more. My intent here is neither to put forth a detailed description of this disorder, nor to discuss its management, for that is better left for medical literature. Yet it is helpful to mention that in the realm of intellectual functions, the events of the remote past are usually preserved in the memory bank of the brain for a longer period of time. On the other hand, the loss in the short term and immediate memory is the most obvious, common and the earliest.

One of the tests performed during the clinical evaluation of such patients, either in the office or at the bedside, is known as Mini-Mental Status Examination or MMSE also called as the Folstein scale. Based on the aggregate responses to this test coupled with other evaluations such as a CT scan, MRI and neuropsychological test, a decision is arrived at by the examiner as to whether the patient qualifies for the diagnosis of Alzheimer's disease or not. And if the individual does suffer from it, the next question oftentimes will be whether a benefit could be derived from specific medications that have recently become available in the past decade or so.

Among the thirty standardized questions that are posed in accordance with this bed side Mini-Mental Status Examination, one question asks the patient to write a meaningful sentence, including a noun and verb. What prompted me to mention about this disorder in fact, relates to the consistency of a rather specific thought expressed through this statement by most of the patients. Whenever such a command is given, the written response that patient often produces on a piece of paper, has always amazed me. It is the same consistent written response "I love my wife" that keeps on coming up time and again, almost in 75% of these elderly individuals. Mind you, most of these patients are in the age group of 65 to 90, a fairly aged population, and the majority of the patients are usually white males.

Such a response is usually not dependent upon the presence of the spouse at the side of the patient. However if the spouse, a wife in most of the cases, was present when an elderly man wrote such a statement, a spark would often glow in her eyes.

Writing this kind of statement shows that on attempting to unclose the doors of human minds that have been closed shut for a while, the verbal expression of love for spouse is still found to be alive and well in the remote files of the memory bank. Such verbal expression of love for the wife or for that matter husband in the face of dwindling intellectual functions - or losing marbles - seems to be relatively more common in the Western patients compared to those of the East.

This selective preservation and then extraction of a specific statement in written language from the vast plethora of many functions in the memory bank seems dependent upon certain fundamental concepts of human behavior. The plausible explanation that makes some sense may relate to the oft-repeated, life-long use of this statement, "Honey! I love you." This verbal expression of love for the spouse is continuously pronounced throughout the life, day in and day out, by almost all the married individuals in the West, so much so that it becomes a conditioned behavior.

The characteristics and influences of this culturally acquired conditioned behavior, to which the human minds have been exposed over a period of time, are thus easier to surface out from within the deep layers of the memory bank when other functions of intellect have sunken deeper. Stuck in the mind in the form of a permanent imprint, it seems not to be easily washed away with the onslaught of old age or by the ravages of this illness. When needed, it becomes readily extractable, not requiring any effort in thinking or use of higher cognition.

This above stated opinion is based primarily on my personal experience over period of time with patients of Alzheimer's disease. Other individuals involved in the management of this disorder may or may not agree on this score and the explanation or hypothesis offered here might not have a scientific basis.

Oftentimes, I wonder if under similar circumstances such a command were to be given to an Indian male, would this kind of answer be written on a piece of paper? This is a million dollar question. Again my personal impression is that Indian men, no matter what part of India they may come from, perhaps would have some difficulty in expressing such feelings, especially in the presence of a third party, such as a physician. The questions then arise, "Why? When other faculties dealing with human behaviors are already altered, why is it that this inhibition in Indian males stays intact in expressing such thoughts openly? What is the cause of such inhibition? Do Indian men not love their spouses as much as men in the West do?"

Again to seek answers to this mystery, one may have to look back to the growth curve of Indians in their indigenous culture. Obviously, this phrase is not used that often in our home culture. Even in their youth, boys and girls in the Eastern culture usually seem to have definite inhibition in openly expressing romance or love, at least in the past. Discussing matters about love, marriage and sex in presence of the elders, have been a taboo, at least when people of my generation were growing up. Writing such a sentence in the presence of a physician - an authoritative figure for an Indian patient - would be considered sexually challenging and hence difficult to spell out or write.

By any stretch of imagination, it shouldn't imply that an Indian will not have any attachment or love for his or her better half. Yet it would be very interesting to interview a large segment of Indians with dementia to determine if they attempt to write an alternate sentence. Having no personal experience with a larger segment of Indian population with dementia, it would be unfair to make a statement one way or the other. Keep in mind, though, that the Indians are a heterogeneous group of people with varied cultures and orientations. Yet, my gut feeling suggests that a response might well turn out to be family-oriented or religion-related.

11.
Unsightly Final Destination

Most of us don't feel comfortable in talking about cremations and burials, especially when we are still young, healthy and live in the so-called 'invincible' United States of America or for that matter in any other advanced countries of the West. Subconsciously, we all keep on hoping that aging and its consequences will somehow not affect us and rather spare us. When our time comes, we hope that medical science will be advanced enough to protect us from the clutches of death. But irrespective of our hopes, the fact remains that all of us will have to face our final moments one day.

In India, the majority of people belong to the Hindu faith. Therefore, it is taken for granted that after the death of an individual, the body will be subjected to cremation as per their established customs and traditions. The Sikh people also believe in the same concept and practice cremation. On the other hand, in the Judeo-Christian culture of the Western world as well as among the Muslims, the burial rather than cremation happens to be the most common method of disposal of human remains, once the light has extinguished from the body.

As cremation is not that common in the West, not much emphasis is placed on it. It is considered to be a poor man's choice. The owners of the funeral homes and cemeteries involved in the funeral business are primarily oriented towards burials and do not take into account the sensitivities and culture of those who believe in cremation. As such, there is not enough business or incentive for the owners of such facilities in the West to spend money in making the surroundings, especially around the incinerators more presentable and dignified. To them, it doesn't make any business sense to be creative for a handful of people. After all, like rest of the world, they too are 'in' for a profit.

Consequently, the facilities for these services such as incinerators are often fragmented and incomplete. If they are available, they are usually substandard at best and their locations and upkeep may not be reasonable. Aesthetically, they may appear unsightly for use as the last place for the permanent disposition of human remains. In stark contrast to the incinerators, the cemeteries are usually well-kept, simply because it is where the real bucks are. While ignorance in the part of operators might well be one of the factors, the major reason for this state of affairs happens to be pure economics like anything else.

Death usually catches many families by surprise. Most of the time, the grieving family is not familiar with what is available and where, making the final process a painful sojourn. The grief due to loss of a loved one is so overwhelming that the issues pertaining to poorly delivered services and the steps required in rectifying them usually take a back seat. However once the time is past, one often tries to forget and leave unpleasant experiences behind, hoping that the people in future will tackle the problems as they face them.

The people from the East have extended families. With a continuous increase in their population in the Western countries, a rise in the number of cremations is obvious. Within the Eastern culture, having as many relatives and friends as possible at the last rites is considered emotionally helpful to the grieving family. Thus despite their small numbers, a relatively good number of individuals show up on such occasion to help support the grieving family. As a consequence, the attendance at the crematorium usually swells up more than what the available facilities could handle. Many of the mourners unfortunately end up standing outside the chapel, unable to join in.

The styles and procedures for religious services among the people of East are usually different from those of the Western perspectives and thus a different kind of setup is required. The prayers and religious hymns for such occasions require a reasonable place to sit on the ground itself. Among Hindus, certain special mantras are read and religious rituals are often performed by specially invited *Pundits* and *Purohits*. In the case of death of a Sikh, a traditional *Shabad Kirtan* consisting of singing *Gurbani*, or reading verses, *Japuji Sahib* and *Kirtan Sohila* as well as *Ardaas* is usually prescribed before cremation. Such rendering is usually performed close to the actual site of cremation and immediately before the body is put into the incinerator.

Despite the increase in the population of people who believe in cremation, I do not believe that it will ever reach a critical mass required by the industry to do something different for us, something that will fit our needs. On the other hand, we also must not forget that after all, not many of us are likely to go back home. Such a thing only exists in our dreams. The cremation being the last stop for our bodies once our souls have taken for a journey to the next world, it makes all the more sense that we must get directly involved in taking a proactive stance to help improve the present situation.

This is a 'matter of life and death' in the literal sense of the words. It is truly one cause in which we all need to bury, No! cremate our hatchets and act together, irrespective of our religious and political affiliations. We all need to sit down and have some cool discussions as to what can and cannot be done to improve the situation.

One option would be to meet with the operators of the mortuaries in the towns we live in. We need to express our desire for improvements in their facilities that would fulfill our needs. The mortuary operators need to be informed that our cultures and religions require neat and clean outdoor ramadas or indoor spaces close to the incinerators. These ramadas or indoor spaces must offer comfortable seating on the floor so that the religious ceremonies can be performed squatting on the floor prior to the body being cremated. There should be elegant landscaping and appropriate decoration conducive to the peace and comfort of the minds of the grieving members of the family.

The surroundings should not give that fearful appearance of the gas chambers of Hitler's Germany that we often see in various WWII movies. Grieving relatives and friends must have sufficient space to stand around the crematorium prior to the body being subjected to the incinerator. This space needs to be well maintained, tidy and appealing to the eyes. It is a common experience that when a body is placed in the incinerator, female relatives become helpless in handling the grief and some of them faint. Therefore, easily available water fountains or bottled water is another thing that could help ease the pain of such occasion.

However, in order to achieve our objectives, we must make realistic proposals, including some incentives so that operators of these facilities could find it in their interest to pay heed to our needs and modify the facilities accordingly. Unless a proposal makes business sense for the operators, it will not work. We need to let them know that our community as a whole will only use a facility that caters to our needs, a facility that is willing to listen and work with us to fulfill our religious and cultural obligations. In turn, we might have to promise to direct all the business from our communities to that location. It might entail some front-end investments by our communities for improving the facility to our specifications and for creating the kinds of environments we wish to have. Interestingly, most of our cremations take place on weekends when cemeteries and burial grounds are not that engaged. This alone should help facility directors to customize the environments to our special needs.

Various Indian organizations in this country seem to be more concerned with the political issues back home. While there is nothing wrong with staying interested in the burning issues of our motherland, the respectful cremation of our remains in foreign lands should also be at the top of the agendas. This can only be tackled by us and us alone.

Nothing will be impossible once we put our minds and souls into it. I sincerely hope that each and every member of the community will give some serious thought to this appeal and join together to do what is right, for this is one issue that concerns us all.

12.

Read This Only, if You Consider Yourself a Mortal

In 2005, in the state of Florida, a prolonged legal drama in relation to life and death was played out openly on the world stage between the husband and parents of a patient, Terri. She was admitted in a long term health care facility and was suffering from a chronic medical condition known as 'Persistent Vegetative State' or "PVS." The continuous battles between her husband on one side and parents on the other, concerning her medical care brought home some painful but pertinent issues, not only for indigenous people but for the diaspora as well. Regardless of one's background and country of origin, one could end up in such a helpless and perhaps lifeless situation like the one Terri was in.

Her situation highlighted a proven yet often forgotten truth that death and disability never discriminate. Yet on the other hand, differences in our perspectives and thought processes that result from our backgrounds and cultures do make us respond differently to a given situation.

People belonging to the Old World tend to procrastinate about several important issues in life, hoping that a divine force will ultimately intervene and somehow spare them the agony. Our Eastern cultures and faiths always reinforce acceptance without complaints for what lies ahead. An attempt to confront or to tamper with the laws of nature is neither encouraged nor it is in our blood. For reasons that are not clear, we seem to extend this philosophy further by simply avoiding any effort to solve issues that seemingly could affect our lives in the most intimate ways.

Terri's case certainly highlighted a critical point that requires our utmost attention. It cautions us that we must openly and clearly decide and declare to ourselves, to the world, and to our near and dear ones as to what should or shouldn't be done, should we end up in situation like the one Terri was in. And this should be done at a time when we are still healthy enough to have our faculties intact. This becomes more imperative in our adopted countries where the laws of our new lands affect us not only while we are alive rather they extend through the process of death and dying and even beyond.

Our value system and our perspectives on the meaning of life are greatly different from those among whom we have chosen to live. For Westerners, many a times 'the life' is often considered an end in itself. The people from the East mostly believe that the time we spend on this earth -- 'the life' as we recognize it -- is a temporary rest stop in the continuous journey of the soul. This temporary rest stop is considered much less important in the Eastern philosophy than what it implies to the Westerners. Over period of time, it is drilled into the psyche of the people of the East that the ultimate destination of the soul lays beyond this life and therefore, all our efforts in life should be directed towards easing its transition to finally merge into 'the power that be.'

The term 'Persistent Vegetative State' became a buzzword during Terri's final weeks and months. The issue of removing the feeding tube from Terri while she was in PVS became a hotly-debated topic in the State of Florida, federal court, and Congress. Even the office of the President of United States didn't stay behind and signed a legislation that allowed Terri's parents to seek a federal judge's review of the case. While the debate was going on, many individuals started to erroneously use the word 'vegetable' instead of 'being in a vegetative state' to describe patients like Terri. For them, the word 'vegetable' and 'being in vegetative state' unfortunately became interchangeable and synonymous. This confusion became a stimulus for me to clarify some of the medical jargons related to PVS.

A 'vegetative state' is a precise medical term for a condition in which the patient appears to be awake but is not aware of his or her surroundings or even own existence. It is a condition of wakefulness without awareness. Such patients cannot think or speak, have no volitional activity, and cannot recognize themselves or their surroundings. It is believed that they do not feel pain because the cerebral cortex and thalamus, the parts of the brain involved with cognitive abilities, are severely damaged.

An attempt at resuscitation following a stoppage or a pronounced irregularity of the heart resulting from a sudden heart attack is the most common cause of this condition. The damaged heart is unable to push the blood to the brain, thereby cutting of the supply of oxygen. Spontaneous cessation of breathing from a myriad of other reasons can also lead to a lack of oxygen flowing to the brain, which again could produce a 'vegetative state.' In medical terminology, such an injury is commonly known as anoxic damage to the brain.

The condition can also be caused by brain injury, bleeding into the brain, stroke and similar maladies. Patients who enter a vegetative state due to a head injury can show some improvement even after a year or so. However, the recovery of the brain from a lack of oxygen as a result of cessation of breathing or sudden heart attack is less common.

In vegetative states, certain vital and automatic functions of the body stay intact, as these functions are under the control of the brain stem, the lower part of the brain that connects the upper brain with the spinal cord. Often patients in this condition have intact eye movements and they maintain full awake-sleep cycles. Acts of grimacing, expressions of discomforts, crying and laughing that are sometimes reported by family members are in reality mere reflexes. Perceptions of pain and suffering are conscious experiences under the control of the higher brain; they disappear when the brain is damaged. Yet the expression of pain can always be elicited involuntarily. The patient is able to breathe independently and the heart continues to pump blood, for such functions are independent of higher brain functions. With the passage of time, patients in vegetative states eventually succumb to death due to other complications, but this does not mean that death always comes quickly.

If a person remains in a vegetative state for approximately three months without any definite improvement, it is then termed a 'Persistent Vegetative State.' This is different from a coma. In a coma, a person is neither aware of the surroundings, nor awake. 'Locked-In Syndrome' is another clinical syndrome with different clinical findings.

Some patients can last in the above-described conditions for decades. Several thousand patients in PVS, in coma, or in 'Locked-In Syndrome' are cared for, at a given point in time, in various nursing homes and hospitals across the United States. These patients cost billions and billions of dollars to the tax-payers annually. With improvements in techniques of resuscitation and artificial support, the number of such cases is constantly on a rise.

Another issue that needs clarification here is brain death, which is often confused with PVS. Brain death simply means what it says; the brain is totally dead, including the brainstem. It is incapable of performing its assigned functions. Heart-circulation activity might persist for as long as two weeks after brain death, though most often it ceases in a matter of hours or days.

Even with the best of intentions of caregivers, taking care of such individuals over an extended period of time becomes emotionally tiring and painfully burdensome. It is here that the dilemma sets in, often putting family members at odds with one another and/or with the medical profession and even with the laws of the land, as was the situation with Terri's case.

An understanding of the legal and ethical issues, as they pertain to 'end of life' situations, is essential. Unfortunately, Terri didn't have an opportunity to make her desires clearly known. Consequently, what her family endured should make all of us pause, think and take initiatives to avoid such scenarios for ourselves and our loved ones. This becomes all the more imperative for those of us who are already climbing the ladders of the 'Golden Years.'

People can establish guidelines under the guidance of physicians by creating advance directives relating to one's terminal healthcare planning. Typically, it involves creating two documents: a 'living will for health' and a 'durable healthcare power of attorney.' By appropriately entering one's wishes into these documents, one can prevent the hassle that Terri's family went through. A 'living will for health' is a document that spells out the wishes of a person about extraordinary medical treatments that could prolong death from terminal conditions like coma and PVS. A 'durable healthcare power of attorney' allows one to assign responsibility to another person, known as an agent, to make all medical decisions about care, including the removal of an artificial feeding tube in situations where the patient is not able to do so.

The 'Do Not Resuscitate' form is another document that requires completion. It clarifies a patient's wishes to the physicians as to how far the resuscitation should be carried through in the case of sudden heart-lung arrest in a hospital setting. The need for such a document is more obvious in patients who are very sick. The physicians taking care of such patients will also need to sign this document. In the absence of these documents, healthcare providers and hospitals must rely on surrogates from the family in an established sequence. If there is an issue, then a guardian has to be appointed by a court and this can then become a lengthy and expensive procedure.

Once these forms have been completed, a copy must be provided to the person who is going to make the decisions. Other family members as well as the physician should have copies of these documents. The documents need to be formally witnessed by someone who is not a beneficiary in the estate and who is not a relative of the patient or involved in the healthcare of patient in question. Sending a copy to the State Attorney General might be beneficial, but such decisions should be taken after proper inquiry into the laws of the State. Under no circumstances, however, should this article be presumed to offer any definitive legal, medical or spiritual advice.

Finally it is imperative that on appropriate occasions, a detailed discussion related to such matters should be carried through with the loved ones in the family. This will help family members become aware of one's wishes. These simple steps usually go a long way in preventing emotionally stressful, financially draining and legally cumbersome burdens on the loved ones. Those left behind will stay truly thankful for such acts of foresightedness.

Note: *Many of the statements and statistics in this essay have been adopted and directly taken from the April 4, 2005, issue of TIME magazine, for which author remains greatly indebted.*

13.

Fair Sex Undermining Fair Sex

A write-up about a somewhat less-than-palatable behavior of the so-called 'Fair Sex' by one belonging to the other side of the aisle (call it 'Unfair Sex' by default) may not be the right thing to do. Yet this matter has been stuck in the convoluted grey matter of my brain for a while, trying to set itself free. Therefore, I finally decided to pull it out in the form of this article.

The issue under discussion here refers to that ever-green and contentious relationship between two females, mother-in-law on one side and daughter-in-law on the other. This less than pleasant relationship between the two isn't something new; rather it has been going on forever, ever since the family unit came into existence. Furthermore at the end of this article, a tangential reference to the exploitation of 'Fair Sex' by members of the same sex, as goes on in one of the oldest professions of mankind, has also been included.

In relation to the first, the unhealthy relationship or bickering between a mother-in-law and daughter-in-law initially takes birth in trivialities. With the passage of time, it gradually turns into open battles. Prior to getting into the thick of matter in the Western world, I, for one thought that this phenomenon was peculiar only to the people of East. But having lived in both the cultures, it is abundantly clear that contentious relationship between mother-in-law and daughter-in-law is equally prevalent in the West. This is irrespective of ethnic backgrounds or places of residence. Whereas a mother-in-law always carries the perception that she is the loser in this game, the newly-wed wife of her son, many times, feels equally slighted.

If it were a plain conflict, one could simply pass it by, but more often than not, the issue of discord may turn into major troubles leading to family and property divisions. Physical injuries as a consequence of attempted suicides and homicides are not entirely unheard of as a consequence of unremitting dispute between the two. The so-called frequent 'stove fires' in the kitchens that lead to the deaths of the newlywed brides in India, as soon as they arrive at the houses of their in-laws are indeed suicides or homicides, as is known to most if not all of us. More often than not, these deaths are the results of unjust demands for dowries put upon the newly-arrived brides by their mothers-in-law. Yet the role of the husbands, fathers-in-law and other members of the family cannot be absolved in such tragedies. The brides are not in positions to force their poor parents to pay for such unnecessary, unjust and excessive demands and finally decide to choose death over continuous slow torture.

One always hoped that with the improvement in overall economy and with the universal spread of education and knowledge, the relationship between mothers-in-law and daughters-in-law in a country like India would finally take a turn for the better. It was believed that the cultural change brought about by the television and movie industry as well as by the free flow of information through education would ultimately bring a change in the situation. The hope was that with the world-wide prevalence and availability of the Internet, the wall of ignorance between them will finally crumble down. It was felt that they would be able to see the world in a fresh light and their insular lives in cocoons will end soon and their interpersonal relations would finally improve.

But unfortunately, this doesn't appear to be the case. In fact, if one happens to watch any sitcom on Indian TV channels, one is given a fairly good dose of the battles that are continuously played out between mothers-in-law and daughters-in-law with much more vigor on each passing day. Looking at the number of sitcoms from Bollywood that keep on churning out - like candies in a factory - and that deal with this subject matter, there doesn't appear to be any letdown in such painful behaviors anytime soon. And if these television shows are representative of anything close to the real life, the undermining of the 'Fair Sex' from itself could continue unabated all the way until the end of this world, at least so it seems. May then God only save the 'Fair Sex' from the 'Fair Sex.'

Even among the people of the West, similar kinds of conflicts are fairly obvious all around. Yet, nothing of the sorts of suicides and stove burning of the brides that unfortunately are so common back home, ever take place here in the West. One important reason for the lack of such menace in the Western countries is the absence of joint-family living arrangements. In fact the system of independent living, a cultural norm in the countries of the West, often prevents occurrences of these kinds of incidents. Another reason is the firm belief in prosecution of perpetrators of such crimes to the fullest extent of the criminal law.

Now let us leave aside these age-old confrontations between a mother-in-law and daughter-in-law for a moment and turn our attention to another social evil that is aided, abetted and sustained by the 'Fair Sex' against its own group. Here I am pointing my finger at the Madams or *'Baais'* in vernacular, the so-called owner-operators of the brothels, where, again, women take full part in hurting their own gender. The so-called Madams of Sins' totally depend upon the ill-gotten earnings from exploitation of the bodies of the 'Fair Sex' for sexual pleasures of men, the 'Unfair Sex.' In fact, this phenomenon has been going on from time immemorial, all over the world irrespective of country and culture.

The situation in the West is not much different than what actually goes on in the countries of the East except that the substrate or commodity, the young prostitute in the Eastern countries, is often poorer, uneducated and naive. The prostitute of the West, on the other hand, is obviously more aware of her rights. Yet the denigration that this profession brings upon the 'Fair Sex' of the West is perhaps the same or even worse as compared to the countries of the East.

The culture in which the 'Fair Sex' falls prey to its own sex is in a dire need of fix. It is time for the activists within the members of the 'Fair Sex' to see the light and attempt to rectify the situation through political and social pressure as well as through education. Unless they truly take it upon themselves and help change the prevailing attitudes and behaviors that have been ingrained in the human mind over centuries, progress will not be likely or easy. If women care not to pay heed, as it seems to be the case since ages, the hope from the male sex, 'the Unfair Sex' unfortunately will be less than unfair, even dismissal.

The job is tough and it needs tougher solutions but left

alone it will get further tough and undoable. The sooner we get the 'Fair Sex' out of this mess, the fairer and better it will be for all. Mothers, sisters, wives and daughters all need to rise up in unison and fight this menace together. Hopefully these humble lines might work as a wake-up call for the 'Fair Sex' and a warning to the 'Unfair Sex.'

.

.

14.

Entertainment:
A Vehicle for Philanthropy

All human beings in this world are not blessed equally. While some have many of the material comforts to live a life full of enjoyment, others might well not even be lucky enough to have their next meal of the day. Guru Nanak Dev Ji, the founder of the Sikh faith, eloquently stated in Guru Granth Sahib Ji, *"Ik Nihaalee Pai Savan ik upar rahan kharhae,"* meaning, "Some may sleep deeply in soft-quilted beds, while others end up standing and watching over them."

All over the world, such kinds of discrepancies are fairly obvious. The majority of people keep their focus and attention to their own needs and try not to concern themselves with the needs of the have-nots. But some, albeit a small number, in almost all the societies of the world, irrespective of their backgrounds, carry this burning desire to help others. These are the ones who usually try to come forward and support various acts of philanthropy. By looking around beyond their horizons, they create opportunities to make this world a better place to live not only for themselves, but for others around them.

It is worth noting here that philanthropy, as many of us have come to know of it, is not an entirely new phenomenon. In fact, a desire to help fellow human beings has always been an integral part of human nature, at least in some, ever since mankind came into being.

In Indian culture, like anywhere else in the world, such acts of philanthropy have been undertaken since ages. The sages and saints of India, the so-called special 'Men of God' always encouraged the Indian community through their spiritual messages to involve themselves in acts of philanthropy. The words of these saintly human beings were considered final and their moral authorities superseded the political authorities of the rulers of their times. These noble souls brought awakening among the masses towards their moral obligations. Their messages and appeals were directed to the inner conscience of ordinary people. They emphasized the need to carry along the poorest of the poor, for those were the ones whom they believed to be closer to God. They took each and every opportunity to speak vehemently against discarding or relegating the poor and the helpless to the bottom of society.

Unfortunately, with modern advances, not many people pay a true credence to or care for such messages. On top of it, the obvious disparity between the needs and resources has made the human beings more self-centered and focused on their own problems. The value systems have changed. With changes in lifestyles, the personal requirements and wants now seem to take front seats and the essential needs of the less blessed ones are pushed onto the back burner.

Moreover, in accordance with the age old truth, 'Out of

sight, out of mind,' many of us who have settled in the West somehow believe that the problems of people back home no longer exist. Living in economically advanced countries, most of the people become financially sound over time and do not come across issues pertaining to the people at the bottom of the totem pole. Such behavior however, doesn't diminish the need for 'giving.'

It is becoming more and more obvious that to fill the economical gap in countries like India philanthropy once again will have to take a more active role. In order to adapt to changing needs and environments of modern times, certain corrections in the way revenues for noble deeds had been collected in the past, will have to be made. There is a need for the people of India to look around in order to pick up the leads from the Western world in using modern means to help arrange needed resources for such acts of philanthropy. With everything going high-tech, one simply cannot depend upon the methods of raising funds in the old ways. The Western style of creating resources for less fortunate fellow human-beings, indeed, turns out to be an inspiration for me to write the following lines.

Fund-raising in Western countries is based on a simple principle that the donor receives something in return for giving. This reciprocity may be in the form of tangible gifts or intangible benefits such as tax deductions, so long giving back is within the domains of the laws of the land. Large high-end dinners, accompanied by entertainment for the donors, happen to be the most prevalent strategy and it seems to be working. But there are other functions - marathons, art shows, and golf tournaments where people contribute money for a noble cause, and have fun doing so. Many different functions in order to promote the causes dear to the donors and to raise funds are often arranged by several charitable organizations as well as by philanthropists.

Attempts are made in the schools from day one to motivate little children to raise monies through different fund-raising activities conducive to their age. Such tasks as making cookies and selling them from door to door, cleaning cars and doing yard work for the elderly in neighborhoods are undertaken by these school going children to help school projects. Students get credit for their classes while fund are raised for a cause deemed necessary by the school community. Chairs named for donors are established for research in the universities. Likewise, research programs in the teaching hospitals for a particular illness are sponsored by rich philanthropists or celebrities who have personally been afflicted by a given illness. It puts a human face on the disease, making people aware of the illness while raising funds for research and education.

Immigrant populations, especially from the Asian countries, possess a cultural tradition that could be melded with philanthropic philosophy. All of us are always busy celebrating one or the other kind of social function with a good number of people attending who always bring gifts for the host, sometimes fairly expensive ones. Several items of food, alcohol and entertainment are always available in plenty. The guests could be requested up-front by the host that instead of bringing those expensive, but not so useful gifts, it would be appreciated if cash could be donated for a cause dear to the host. One may think that it looks odd and out of place to request money from the guests who have been invited to have a good time. But eventually people will start accepting this trend simply because the amount donated would be usually far less than what is often spent on those hefty gifts. The way it is now, the gifts that are brought in by the guests usually end up into the garages or basements of the hosts, collecting dust. It is however essential to recognize that such requests will work only if the use of money is appropriate and transparent with clear-cut objectives that are conducive to the psyche of all those who happen to attend such functions.

At the next party by another host, a different project could be designated to be recipient of such efforts. Indeed there are many projects intrinsic to the needs of people in home countries that could take advantage of such acts of philanthropy through the funds collected by these gatherings. Road improvements, segment by segment, establishment of dispensaries and school betterment projects in the hometowns of NRIs, could all be designated as beneficiary of such collections. Donating to religious institutions is important but is also a very personal decision. NRIs from the West could personally play a constructive role by arranging functions for philanthropic acts while they are visiting their home countries.

Understandably, those starting their careers and those with young families do have a need to establish themselves first. What is important, however, is to keep in mind that philanthropy simply isn't limited to donating money. Many among us possess special skills in our chosen professions. One can always find ways and means to help people in need yet with our own styles and skills. People in the medical profession have certainly much to offer. Likewise, the individuals with governmental agencies could teach their fellow brethren back home about the structure and operations of their departments in the West and guide them in acting responsibly in timely fashion to meet the needs of the people they are supposed to serve. Teachers may share their skills in relation to their profession as practiced in the West. Those in business could spend time with their counterparts to train them in the Western style of the customer service.

By such deeds, our stay in these Western countries will not only become useful to us but equally to the near and dear ones we left behind. In fact if it wasn't for those at home who truly invested in us during times of our need, we wouldn't be where we are today. It is now our turn to try our best to use our resources to pay back our loved ones and elevate their standard of living, improve their lifestyle and bridge the gap of disparity. *Keep in mind though, that life is short, time is less, needs are plenty and immediate action is of the essence.*

15.
The Job of a Physician is to Entertain a Patient while an Illness Runs its Course

The title of this essay basically implies what was once said by Voltaire, a well-known 18th century French philosopher, writer and poet. For those of us in the business of medicine, this statement might appear to be somewhat disconcerting but the truth behind it becomes fairly obvious if one looks at it objectively.

The miracles of medical science have conquered many skies and oceans and much that lies in between. Over the last century, medical science has grown exponentially. Physicians have learned to treat and defeat many horrible diseases that in the past were untreatable. New therapies and innovations in surgical procedures have succeeded in ways that are beyond comprehension. Our lives have become much more comfortable than those of our predecessors, thanks to an incomparable era of medical progress.

Examples of the progress of medical science are fairly obvious in every medical discipline. One of the best-known examples is bypass surgery for blocked coronary arteries of the heart. This surgery helps patients avoid life-threatening heart attacks, allowing them to enjoy many more years of life. Other examples include the removal of obstructions in arteries that take blood to the brain, thus preventing future brain strokes. The medical management of arthritis has brought much-needed relief to countless sufferers of chronic pain and disability. Furthermore, the replacement surgeries for joints, especially those for hips and knees, indeed provide a new lease on life for patients in need.

Not long ago, the role and status of a physician was considered to be next to that of a God, if not God's equal. A physician's words were accepted as final and no questions were ever asked. Accordingly, people used to put their full faith in their healers. The patients and the unsuspecting public at large trusted the medical profession so much that they often felt that physicians could and would do almost anything to treat and cure them.

However, under such environments the distinction between treatment and permanent cure was almost completely blurred. Part of the confusion was related to the way medical information was disseminated to the public. More often than not the information was allowed to filter out in such a way that it aided and abetted the medical profession more than it helped the patients.

Though universal, this phenomenon was more common in the countries of Asia and Africa where the general public was poorly educated and susceptible to being misled by untrained and unqualified healthcare providers. Aggressive and over-bloated commercialism by the medical profession was fairly common. Even now, one notices the same kind of stories, advertisements, and announcements in ethnic TV channels and newspapers all over the world. One often comes across claims of miraculous treatments and cures that could turn a patient into a whole new person in a week or so, regardless of their problems. But these claims are usually not proven by the facts. Rather, they quickly fizzle under close scrutiny.

Yet for all of our advances, there are many intricacies of the human body which we do not fully comprehend. The causes and best treatments for many ailments still elude us, defying science and all of our efforts. Physicians, nurses, and others in the medical field recognize that they are often helpless, and that no 'miracle cure' is on the horizon for several ailments, regardless of their best efforts. In many respects, we are still stuck in situations that make us realize that Voltaire was not off the mark after all. To that end - being a physician myself - I am willing to bear testimony to the great truth that Voltaire pronounced, but with a few exceptions.

We all know that surgeons can cut and remove unwanted, unhealthy and diseased organs from the body and replace them with artificial devices. Yet such devices are not the ones that ultimately help in healing. Once the knife of a surgeon places a cut on the human body or an antecedent trauma leads to the injury, the job of a surgeon merely remains limited to approximating the edges of the cut by stitches. This approximation hastens the ultimate closure of the cut or the wound and prevents it from getting infected by bacteria. The setting of a fracture in proper alignment is the job of an orthopedic surgeon, but the process of healing between the two broken segments of a bone is not under his or her control. Similarly, after a joint is replaced artificially, it is not the surgeon that heals the joint. Physical therapy definitely helps in expediting the process of recovery, but this is not the end of the story. In each case, nature has to chip in to finish the job.

Transplanting a body organ is one thing, but to make a transplant work is not up to the physicians. Acceptance of the transplanted organ requires the intervention of the hand of nature, albeit with the help of drugs to prevent its rejection by the immune system of the recipient. Likewise, a brain stroke leaves a person with significant neurological deficits, sometimes including paralysis of certain parts of the body or loss of speech and/or vision. Here again, it is the natural resilience of the body that determines the final outcome, although interventions by aggressive physical therapy, speech therapy, or visual rehabilitation certainly act as a booster. The same is true for a patient after having a heart attack.

The lay press and media, at times, have been noted to advertise that such and such provider can permanently cure a patient of cancer. Such advertisements fail to mention that not all cancers are lethal. If left alone, patients with certain kinds of growths can improve themselves over a period of time. Likewise, in the realm of conservative medical managements, many illnesses heal themselves with time. Many of us are all too familiar with this oft-quoted statement in the medical profession. *"Medicine can cure a cold in a week, while doing nothing will heal it within seven days."* Once again, it is the built-in resilience of the human body that kicks in over a reasonable period of time and under proper environments. Of course, the prerequisite of knowing about the benign nature of the illness is paramount and should not be ignored. But when untrained and unscrupulous medical professionals start taking credit for the cure of self-healing illnesses, it simply becomes a fraud.

My purpose here is not to denigrate the trained health care providers, nor do I question the effectiveness of proven science. Rather, I simply wish to highlight and clarify what Voltaire said so many years ago. There is a place for medicine to intervene, and then there is a place for one's natural body defenses to take over under the supervision of watchful professionals. There is no need to replace one with the other, as both are interdependent and not mutually exclusive. Working in tandem and seeking the help of the medical profession when needed, while fully understanding the imperfections of medical science, ultimately leads to a correct path. The awareness of the deficiency of science will help create a ripe environment for progress by bringing forth the impetus for mankind to look beyond, through further scientific research. At the same time it helps ordinary public realize the difference between a fact and a fiction.

16.
'Respondez S'il Vous Plait'

'Respondez s'il vous plait,' sounds French, right? Yes, it is French indeed! In fact those popular four letters, 'RSVP' that we so often read at the bottom of each and every invitation, happen to be an abbreviation of the heading written above in French. Translated in English, it means, 'Please Respond.' What a humble and wishful request on the part of a host of a given event.

Yet, it is a common experience that many of the lucky ones who receive such invitations care not to respond back. Of the myriad of explanations given for such attitudes, this one is fairly prevalent, "Too much was going on at that moment, so we didn't have time to say yea or nay. And finally when we came to realize, it was too late."

Sometime back a beautiful essay on this topic, penned by Emily Seftel, appeared in the 'Arizona Republic,' a daily newspaper in Phoenix, Arizona. The way that article was written became a motivation for this write-up.

Contrary to the common perception that such a casual behavior could only be a manifestation of procrastination within some members of the diaspora, it turns out that this disease is widespread. It seems not to discriminate between race, ethnicity or culture. It was indeed a rude awakening to realize that people of the West, who otherwise tend to be meticulous in their appointments and schedules, become equally apathetic, if not more than the people of Eastern background, when it comes to responding back to the host. Such a phenomenon does not spare even the so-called elites of Western society. The prevalence among them by no means falls short of the common man. Receiving an invitation and not calling back is something that seems to be built-in among human beings all over the world.

Up until half a century ago, the host of a planned event in India would try to visit the invitees to deliver a personal invitation. With a personal encounter, it would become apparent at the time of a visit whether a prospective invitee will grace the occasion or not. A need to respond at a later date, for all practical purposes, was unnecessary. Then came a time when these personal invitations became even more formal. In addition to just delivering the invitation, the host would carry along boxes of sweets or fruits. The outcome would again become known right there and then and nothing was ever left to the whims of the guests.

With the passage of time, we started dragging the post office into the business of delivering invitations. Sending invitations through the mail became somewhat imperative as the number of guests increased and the distances prevented people from personally traveling to each household. With this method, however, the number of the guests that finally showed up for the event was always left in limbo to the last moment. The poor host could only find out at the eleventh hour as to who would grace the occasion and who would not. Then along came the Internet and e-mails. This method became the medium of choice for young and computer-savvy individuals. Gradually, this change became more popular within the masses in view of its ease and now it seems to have taken over all the other means of communication. The other advantage of this method is that it doesn't take much effort on the part of the invitee to respond back, provided one is motivated to do so.

When a person invites a guest, it simply implies that not only does the host care for the invitee but considers him or her worthy of the utmost respect to include such a person on the list. By putting RSVP on the invitation, the host is simply seeking to find out the intentions of the guest. Showing apathy in not responding back leads to many annoying and unfortunate consequences both for the host as well as the invited guest.

The most pressing concern pertains to the preparation of the food. Having no idea as to how many guests will finally show up, unfortunately leaves the host undecided about the exact arrangements. No host on earth would ever like to be embarrassed if the food were to fall short. On the other hand, preparing food in plenty in anticipation of a large number of invited guests, who might decide not to show up at the eleventh hour, brings a poor taste among those who had spent their precious efforts and time. Moreover, the empty tables or chairs that were supposed to be graced by the esteemed guests, indeed, turn the joyful moment into a disgraceful, unpleasant and unsavory experience for all concerned.

The other side of the coin is equally important. Within the diaspora it has been noticed that some of its members, at times, try to tag along an uninvited friend and family member to the event. Etiquettes demand that any guest that has shown up, invited or uninvited, must be treated with equal respect and made to believe that his or her presence is fully appreciated. Therefore, hosts will often go out of their ways to welcome such unexpected guests and make them a part of the joyful occasion. Unfortunately those who bring uninvited persons ignore the fact that events arranged at expensive places, where each and every seat is worth hundreds of dollars, may cost bundles to the host in the final tab. Likewise, some of the diaspora members do not hesitate to bring their little children along. Children being children, they don't change and invariably run around and make mess of everything that comes their way, turning a nice party into mayhem. The poor hosts are thus put in a great bind, for they could neither stop nor encourage such uninvited accompaniments.

Several strategies to help avoid such a scenario are possible but all have their own shortcomings. Soft notes, giving hints to the prospective guests against bringing small children along with, could be added to the invitation. A simple statement on the invitation, mentioning that this event is limited to adults above a certain age might do the trick. But more often than not it doesn't work, for each person considers his or her children to be special and not like those of the others.

Therefore, it is important to be specific when sending out invitations. Some of the hosts may openly declare their inability in accommodating children in the planned celebration, seeking an up-front apology that is clearly stated on the invitations. A few others might end up specifically mentioning the names of the guests whom they intend to invite, like 'In favor of Mrs. ..... and Mr. .....' The word 'family' is not written or printed after the name of the guests. Once the word 'family' goes on the invitation, one must be ready to accommodate any number of the guests. Gone are the days when the diaspora families were small, consisting of a husband and wife. Now with children and their children and then many of their close relatives, the families have expanded all around. With a continuous ongoing trickle of several relatives and friends visiting from back home, many diaspora members now have fairly large extended groups of household members, making it imperative to specify the names or number of people one wishes to invite.

What is most important but often forgotten is that an invitation happens to be a unique privilege afforded to the invited guest. It should not be taken by the guest as a mere ritual. It is a well-known fact that a self-addressed stamped envelope always arrives with the invitation. The advantages in creating goodwill and maintaining relationships through a simple response within a reasonable time frame will always be worth the effort. Not playing the game within the rules and not responding back within the specified time-period is tantamount to a lack of understanding of this basic concept. Not only does it belittle the host or the hostess but it insults them deeply much akin to a slap on their faces. Nothing should be done either through an act of simple omission or commission to lose previously established steady contacts.

17.
Individuals vs. Institution: East vs. West

The Eastern immigrants, after arriving at the Western shores, usually become exposed to a new sociopolitical environment that is entirely different from what they had previously experienced while living in their home countries. In fact, this new style of environment as well as the governance may be one hundred eighty degrees apart from the one they had in their motherlands.

The West, as we all know, puts its emphasis on a democratic style of government that relies heavily upon certain sets of norms. As time passes, such norms become standardized and institutionalized. All of the decision-making processes then start working through these established institutions. The individuals, even if they wish to modify any practice, rule or law, have to depend upon the relevant institutional processes and procedures. An emphasis on a small group of people or on one person, irrespective of one's political-economical muscle, is thus avoided. This process has been helping Western nations and their citizens avoid falling prey to the tentacles of a few individuals who often refuse to give up power, as is seen in some countries of the East or in Africa.

For quite sometimes, the sociopolitical environments of the countries of the East catered to the whims of their rulers. Even if the 'men in power' were originally elected democratically, they often refused to abdicate their thrones. Rather, they simply remained stuck to their chairs because there was no institutional pressure for them to do otherwise. They tried their best to stay in power and to keep the seats warm for their ego as well as for their progeny, so that their legacies - good and not-so-good - could be carried out long-term. It didn't bother them to ignore or violate the established norms of whatever minimal political institutions their countries might have had. In many of the so-called 'young democracies' of the East, the 'democracy' quickly recoiled under pressure, thanks to the muscle flexing power of the 'men in power.'

In the history of India, such phenomenon has been occurring for centuries. One really does not need to turn back too many pages of history to unravel such behaviors of the politicians of India, past and present. Each and every chapter is full of painful examples. However, the intent is not to unclose those painful chapters to perform a political post-mortem here, rather to emphasize the fundamental difference in the political and social cultures of the East and West.

The Indian people, by and large, are subservient, obedient, supportive and respectful to the individuals in authority, often at the expense of country's institutional frame–work. They will cater to the 'men in power' or the authority so long as such men belong to their own tribes, castes, villages, cities or states, irrespective of their qualities and qualifications and regardless of their lack of interest towards the concept of the institution. When the entire thrust is put behind the individuals, the respect for institutional principles is often ignored. At the same time, for all practical purposes, the person in power often considers him or her as the only and the total authority and tries to act like an institution in itself and doesn't feel any obligation to abide by established norms.

The ordinary citizens of many countries of the East have been conditioned in such thinking over long periods of time. Public institutions as foundations for law and governance, constitute somewhat of an abstraction for them. Although established institutions are truly meant to preserve and enhance the strength of a government, not much emphasis is placed upon them by the people of the East in some cases. As a result, these institutions, per se, don't seem to have much authority or significance.

Such attitudes on the part of the citizens did not appear in one day, a month, or even a year. Rather, they became ingrained in their minds over a long period of time. It is the consequence of centuries of absolute rule by an unending succession of kings, queens and emperors and then the foreign nationals, none of whom ever practiced anything even close to 'democracy.'

When an immigrant lands at the shores of a Western country for the first time, he or she is faced with a dilemma to make a choice between the two systems. The imprints of previous experiences are already deeply rooted into the psyche of newly arriving immigrants and are, therefore, permanent. This is much like an automobile's odometer that contains a good amount of previously logged-in mileage. On the other hand, the system of governance that the immigrant now faces, opens up channels that are totally different and yet appealing.

For a while, the immigrant does not have a clear-cut picture of what is right and what is wrong. It becomes difficult to determine which of the two styles of political systems one should follow, as the familiarity with the old clashes with the opportunities of the new. The thought process, at least in some individuals, starts swinging like a pendulum between the newer democratic system that places emphasis on institution and the past experience of the authoritarian type of government back home.

People born and raised in most of the countries of the West, especially the U.S., Canada and Western Europe do not confront such issues. In their minds, the concept of a true institution, whether it relates to government or society, is fixed deeply for this is the only system to which they have been exposed. The Western governments usually tend not to force their will upon ordinary people, even if they have political power. Through their past experiences, such governmental agencies become fully aware that wielding excessive power could easily land them in trouble, more likely sooner than later. Unlike certain governmental authorities of the East, it is not lost on them that the positions of power and authority they have attained are indeed temporary. They seem to understand fully that their existence in an institutionalized political system is based upon democratic principles. They are mostly aware that the supremacy and permanence of the institutional system is here to stay, regardless of how much political power or strength they as individuals or a group might have emulated during their terms in the office.

Additionally, the people of the West are fully cognizant that their diverse lifestyles have been constantly influenced by the heterogeneity derived and fueled by the intermixing of people from different nations, cultures, ethnicity and heritage.

It is fairly obvious to them that their unique way of living is a manifestation of the thought process developed under multi-cultural, multi-ethnicity and multiple-faith influences. They also seem to accept this reality that it is a manifestation of their past open-door policy towards immigration that created and supported diversity, which in turn brought all the richness and abundance to their societies. They understand it fully well that, as a consequence, it is unlikely that the pendulum of power will ever swing back towards a few individuals, irrespective of their economic, social or political status.

While the culture and method of governance in the West provides more individual freedom, yet in acknowledging this fact, it becomes imperative for newly-arrived immigrants to keep their eyes open to face new ground realities. They need not lose sight of the fact that the sociopolitical structure of the West represents a major change for them. It may take a long time for them to understand and accept the Western perspective on governance. But once the reality sets in, it becomes obvious that the political institutions of the West do have their advantages. The immigrants eventually start understanding that the 'men in power' in their home countries, to whom they had been subservient all their lives and paid their honest and undivided dues, were no more than mere mortals like others.

The kings and queens of the past did what they did because ordinary men like us allowed them to do so. Once these haughty mortals left the scene, their authorities and the fear complexes that they instilled in the minds of the public at large also washed away with them. Left are the historians only, who end up writing mere footnotes about their kingdoms and whatever little else, if any, they achieved during their rules.

On the other hand, the well-established institutions based

123

on democratic principles, where the will of the people is given an upper hand, usually stay supreme and remain untouched for ever. *History teaches us and modern times prove it that a government dependent upon the whims of an individual, no matter how strong or able such an individual might well have been, ultimately ends up seeing a doom's day.*

18.
Square Pegs, Round Holes

In order to make a square peg fit snugly in a round hole, a good amount of effort is required. Either edges of the pegs have to be smoothened out or else the round hole will require widening, otherwise it is unlikely that the square-shaped peg will fit snugly in that round hole.

The lifestyle of an immigrant from the Eastern world, fully pregnant with the well-established cultural traditions of his or her homeland, can be easily compared to that of the square peg mentioned above. The untested environment of new adopted country and its dominant alien Western culture is akin to a round hole in this example. The peg with its sharp edges – the previous cultural lifestyle of an immigrant – will have to be smoothened out implying that such lifestyle will have to be unlearned somewhat. Then and only then, the round hole will allow the entry of the peg meaning, that the alien Western culture will let an immigrant settle comfortably.

The question that unfolds here relates to whether smoothening of the edges of the peg also implies foregoing one's culture completely or compromising the fundamentals of one's Eastern faith and identity in order to live in a new society or country? In my way of thinking, neither of the conditions has to be a prerequisite for achieving such an objective. It certainly means, however, that there is a serious need to look into the pattern of our intrinsic thought processes and habits. Realignment with the prevalent culture, albeit only to the extent that doesn't erode such concepts of one's faith and moral values of the previous culture, may be justifiable and should be seriously considered. Painful as it might well be to accept this fact, it needs to be realized however, that such issues require an open mind. Choosing what is best among both the cultures should be the ultimate goal.

A few scattered examples here and there taken from other articles in this anthology might further clarify the issues under discussion. In total contrast to the time-tested cultural wisdom, we now seem to hesitate and find it relatively difficult to open our pockets to pay for something, especially, if personal gains in a deal are not obvious to us. In doing so, we somehow try to reconcile and justify to ourselves that wasting money is the Western way and not what our culture calls for. On the other hand, most of us didn't care enough about accumulating materialistic possessions back home; in part, because there wasn't much at stake in many cases. And even if it were, our religious and cultural environments, kept on continuously hammering upon us, the elements of satisfaction and sharing. Many among us were always ready to spend whatever little we could afford, if we found or felt that the project at hand was useful to someone in the society or to ourselves.

But all of a sudden on entering into this culture, both tangible and intangible gains start taking full control of our psyche. This may happen, as a consequence of rapid onslaught of materialistic ideology that surrounds us as soon as we land here and then finally overtakes the better of us.

Take, for instance, the advice given by a physician. If that advice does not come with something corporeal, such as bagful of prescription medications, it bothers us to pay for it. A dermatologist spends his entire career differentiating between cancerous and non-cancerous lesion through visual inspection. He or she doesn't command the same kind of respect as a surgeon, simply because the later uses knife in removing the cancer in a dramatic way. We do not hesitate to mention that all what the dermatologist did was to cast one look at the skin and bill so much for it. It is simply forgotten that had the dermatologist not diagnosed the lesion correctly, the surgeon wouldn't have been able to operate on it and remove it.

Consider another example. During O. J. Simpson's trial, his attorney Johnnie Cochran used this statement "If it doesn't fit, you must acquit" referring to the glove that O. J. was presumably wearing at the time of murder. O. J. would have become history, vanishing slowly behind bars for the rest of his life, had this statement been not used by his attorney. No amount of remuneration will ever be enough for this intangible statement that O. J.'s attorney made at that crucial juncture which ultimately saved his life. Instead O. J. ended up getting away only with that infamous non-guilty verdict.

Let us now look at another issue. In this culture, it is usually believed that one enjoys food by sight, not necessarily because of taste. No doubt the nutritional value of the food as well as where and in what surroundings it is prepared and served, all happen to be important. Yet the ambiance of a restaurant is what makes a restaurant most pleasing to the eyes and hence ultimately popular and successful in the West.

People from East, on the other hand, tend to have a different attitude. We seem to care less for the ambiance and more for our taste buds that over many years have been accustomed to the flavors of various spices and condiments. In fact this is one reason that roadside '*Dhabas*' have become the lifeline of the Indian culture in relation to eating out, never mind their poor aesthetic surroundings. 'Indian spicy food' seems to be the motto among many of us, notwithstanding where and how that food is served.

We do not mind paying for tasty food but the service provided by a waiter or waitress doesn't carry much weight in our eyes. Leaving a fair amount of tip is considered somewhat wasteful and bothersome to some, especially the recent arrivals among us. To a Western-born and grown-up individual, paying a good amount of tip consistent with the service is the norm of life and is considered a part of an enjoyable restaurant experience.

Here I am also reminded about the attitude of some members of Sikh congregations towards the *Raagis* or the religious singers in the Gurdwaras of the West. Oftentimes, it is questioned by some as to why the religious singers are paid so much when their duty to sing in Gurdwaras usually doesn't exceed one or two hours a week. Somehow it is ignored that this one hour of performance just couldn't have happened like that. In fact, behind that hour, there usually is consistent training of many years, sometimes from early childhood, and that too by individuals who are intuitively blessed and religiously oriented. Had the same person under similar circumstances, taken to a lifestyle of a pop-singer instead, he or she could have made a tremendous amount of money and gained significantly in material comforts?

I vividly remember an incident that might further clarify the difference in our thinking as opposed to that of a Western-born and raised individual. An India-born Sikh questioned an American-born Sikh woman about the futility of spending so much money every Sunday on expensive fresh flowers for the decoration in front of Sri Guru Granth Sahib Ji. This India-born person wanted to know, why one could not simply use silk flowers instead and save money by not buying fresh flowers every Sunday. According to him, the quality silk flowers looked equally beautiful and didn't require frequent changes, thus avoiding unnecessary expenses of Gurdwara funds. The amount saved could be wisely used for some other constructive needs, so he felt.

The response from the American-born Sikh woman was truly an eye opener. "There is no bigger gift than presenting fresh flowers to the one whom you consider the most deserving of your respect or love. The silk flowers or for that matter the flowers made of gold will not be equivalent to the bouquet of fresh fragrant flowers. And for a Sikh, Guru Granth Sahib Ji, the Guru Eternal, is the one whom one would wish to pay the utmost respect in one's life."

Another interesting point worth considering here relates to the enjoyment of idle time and vacations. Taking vacations for many of us in our past culture was often considered a kind of chore. And even if some of us could afford them, we ended up making visits to religious places. Nothing was wrong in such an attitude for this was what our lifestyle, culture and faith dictated. This is in total contrast to the thought process of the majority of the people among whom we have decided to settle. Vacations here, most of the time, are considered to be vacations from every assignment, religious included. Yet after being part of the Western culture for many years, our affinity for spending vacations at religious places still refuses to leave many of us and perhaps for good spiritual reasons!

One could go on and on and enumerate countless such examples where the difference in the thought process becomes so obvious between the people born and raised in two different cultures.

The question under consideration then is, how can we change our attitudes and behaviors so that we maintain the goodness of our back home traditions while not sounding or acting as if we are out of place in this culture? The answer perhaps lies in a keen sense of observation and then discrimination as to what happens around us and how indigenous people act or behave in a given situation. This may to some extent get us into a habit of doing things in an appropriate way. One must remember though that everything we did in the past back home might not have always been necessarily appropriate or desirable. Likewise, to accept every action in total, the way it is practiced here, cannot always be considered right or in our best interest.

Another way to learn would be to look at the attitudes and behaviors of our children growing up here. They provide us with a ready-made combination of both the cultures. Certainly they might not always make the choices we would. Yet their lifestyles and behaviors do have something to offer to us. Paying attention to the subtleties they exhibit in their attitudes might benefit us greatly. At the same time, their growth pattern provides us with an opportunity to guide them through, should we observe something off the mark.

All in all, our lives will become more productive, pleasant and less problematic if we keep ourselves in a learning mode rather than staying fixed on the behaviors and attitudes we brought with us from back homes. The individuals who keep an open mind to the situations around them will be the ultimate winners in this complex and somewhat alien culture. The 'square pegs' will certainly fit snugly into the 'round holes' once we have done the homework to smooth the edges. Only then will we fit snugly in the culture in which we have decided to surround ourselves.

19.

Replacing a Spouse When One Foot is Already in the Grave

Drops of water, if allowed to fall uninterruptedly on a hard rock for a long period of time, will ultimately cause erosion of that rock. Likewise, if one is continuously surrounded by a culture that is intrinsically foreign to the social and moral values of that individual, a certain amount of change in the cultural behavior is likely. This will occur no matter how strong or diagonally apart one's previous culture and traditions might have been and irrespective of how small or great the divide between one's native culture and the culture of the adopted land happens to be. Such elements of new environments ultimately influence the individual in all spheres of life.

The people of the East, after migrating to the West and establishing their permanent abodes, gradually begin a transition in their lifestyles. Such metamorphosis in their day-to-day social lives, an outcome of the altered environment, is not that easy yet it is understandable simply because the basic survival is the utmost and first issue in their minds. Otherwise the sailing could not be smooth. There is a dire need, however, for a fine discrimination in this matter in relation to how far one can or should go with the flow. Therefore, a true and good working understanding of one's past culture, traditions and values becomes essential in facilitating a transition to a new culture.

The issue in this write-up refers to a particular change in the lifestyles of some members of the diaspora that doesn't seem to fit well with the established norms of their previous Eastern culture. The phenomenon of replacing or discarding a spouse for simple insignificant reasons or carrying a desire to do so, after having lived together for several years, seems to be showing its ugly head gradually, as time passes. As of yet, it has been practiced by only a very small number of members, primarily the males. Still, we need to pay heed to this issue, for otherwise the slippery slope upon which this travel begins can lead to a downfall in the dark and deep hole of doom for those who take that route.

"*Aik Jott Doaiye Moorti*" meaning "two bodies with one common internal energy or light," is the underlying concept of the union between man and woman, as was preached and practiced all around us in our Eastern cultures. The marriage, having taken place between two individuals, is considered to be a 'once and for all' deal. It is always emphasized that the spousal relationship is pre-ordained and once solemnized could not be discarded or changed at will for trivialities. Therefore, the phenomenon of replacing or discarding a spouse has not been in vogue in Eastern cultures in the past.

After migrating to the Western countries, and for reasons that are fairly obvious, this socio-spiritual message gets easily diluted and the vows taken at the time of the wedding seem not to carry much weight in the minds of those who wish to take a plunge against them. The clever human mind starts finding ways and means to justify the futility of such vows. Among members of the diaspora, one of the most common reasons to seek a separation or divorce is the alleged incompatibility between the couple. Once this thought takes hold, fissures start widening, a weakening of the relationship follows and undoing of the knots becomes the ultimate goal. But such a reason for a change in behavior, as put forth by the individuals who try to follow this course, doesn't appear to be rational, especially if considered from the Eastern perspectives.

This concept of 'incompatibility' was not commonly acknowledged in India. The incompatibility, if it actually occurred, usually showed up in the early phases of marriage. And if it was of a serious nature, the couples oftentimes looked to the elders of the family in order to sort out their differences. Social pressure was so acute that even to think in another direction was considered a sin. Faced with a situation where the resolution of the conflict appeared impossible, the concerned friends and relatives would not object to the breakdown of that marriage given the fact that it still was in the early phases. If the chemistry between the husband and wife didn't take hold to begin with or the spark didn't ignite early in the marriage, 'nothing will change' was the *mantra* that guided the elders as well as the couples concerned.

What seems to be different here in the West is the appearance or pronouncement of so-called incompatibility at the later stage of life by the dominant member himself especially at a time when his one foot is already nearing the grave. Unfortunately such a behavior doesn't imply a true incompatibility. In fact it is a manifestation of lust, loose moral values or greed that oftentimes turns out to be the underlying factor in seeking a replacement for the weaker spouse in such situations. Leaving grown-up children and grandchildren high and dry late in one's life, for the simple fulfillment of less-than-honorable intentions, is not only plain awkward, it is awfully painful. And to hide such a need under the garb of 'incompatibility' and use it as defense for such actions and that too after a lifetime of togetherness is simply deplorable.

In the Eastern culture, when a spouse passes away, the vacuum is easily filled by the members of the extended-family. In order to ward off the grief, the children and grandchildren come forward to cover the loss and thus the pain of loneliness is lessened. In the West, on the other hand, a need for companionship for the lonely surviving partner, if the children have already left the nest, assumes different proportions and becomes significant. No fair-minded person can dispute such a need, and a yearning for a true and stable companionship becomes justifiable under such circumstances.

There is another aspect of life in the West that needs attention. With the frequency of interracial marriages rising all around, one partner - usually the female - turns out to be native-born belonging to the indigenous majority group while the male partner is usually from the Eastern culture. Such mixed interracial couples may be very close-knit initially, but with the passage of time, they end up developing difficulties in relationships. While the partner from the local majority naturally relates to the local environments and majority culture, the alien male partner usually remains mentally immersed in his previous home culture. Finally one fine morning, sometimes even after a quarter of century or more, the indigenous partner seeks a break in the relationship. The reason given is just simple and plain tiredness or 'incompatibility.' Such discord might appear to be trivial to begin with but ultimately it leads to grave outcome.

It is said that *"marriages are made in heaven but are consummated on earth."* This sounds true at the time of the wedding, for at that moment love mixed with attraction and lust tends to supervene. But when the flames of so-called "fire of love" start dwindling, even after the addition of more and more fuel and rekindling, the couple may decide that it is not worth any more to keep on tagging along. While the exact statistics of such incidences are not available, some mixed couples in the Asian diaspora seem to have suffered such a fate, especially at a later date in their marriages.

What one should wish and try to practice whole-heartedly is to make honest efforts in attempting to keep this most pious relationship cemented forever by practicing their initially promised slogan "together, till death do us part." The Eastern culture and faiths always put great emphasis and efforts in trying to drill such moral convictions deep into the psyche of its people. However, when one decides to leave the native culture, the need to fully respect, honor and follow those golden principles should not be tossed aside simply because the location for the remaining breaths of life has merely changed.

SQUARE PEGS, ROUND HOLES

.

20.

Laddoos vs. Aansoos

Throughout history, nomadic (hunter-gatherer and herding) and agricultural societies have consistently placed more stock in males. Over thousands of years, this attitude of male-gender superiority has become rooted in the cultural traditions of such societies.[1] Despite enough efforts in educating people about the importance of gender equality, we the Indians and other people of Eastern backgrounds still continue to give greater status to the male gender. It shouldn't be forgotten however, that the concept of male superiority was just as prevalent in European and American cultures as in the Eastern cultures. With the onslaught of industrialization in the West, gender roles began to change. In many aspects of life, women gained equality or near-equality with men.

Industrialization did take place in India too, and technological know-how has obviously made great strides in turning Indian culture upside-down. But rather than bringing woman to relative equality, we began using modern technology to wipe her out from the very face of this earth, right at birth and often before she could even see the light of day. The ultrasound machines that were meant to diagnose illness and save human lives were put into killer modes instead, silencing that tiny, unborn female heartbeat ticking in its mother's womb. I am referring to the degrading, inhumane and outright evil custom of female feticide or the non-therapeutic abortion for female fetus. Female feticide is a custom that continues to flourish unabated in certain parts of India, especially in Punjab. Because of such behavior, the Punjabis have earned the dubious distinction of being one of the foremost groups in India that are most likely to commit such a heinous crime. The difference between them and the other groups that encourage this practice is the mere factor of hypocrisy.

In many respects, the attitude of Indians could be considered akin to that of an oily surface that never gets wet regardless of how heavy it might rain. We do not consider for a moment that all the good things that we enjoy in life are, in large part, consequences of the efforts and sacrifices made by our women-folks. Women's contributions to every facet of life are equal to, if not greater, than men yet somehow we always manage to take them for granted.

The workload of an ordinary woman in India is much greater than that of a man. Like a machine, she is often busy all day, every day and seven days of the week and the entire 365 days of the year. There is no such thing as a vacation for her and there is no provision for rest. Even machines are turned off once in a while to cool them off and to have routine maintenance. But alas, such is not the case for the woman of the house. Her work entails taking care of the entire household from sunrise to sunset and even beyond to the midnight. Included among her chores is cooking for the entire family, doing dirty laundry and then helping the rest of the family members in their physical work in the fields or wherever else. Yet first her father, then brothers followed by her husband and finally her sons, the so-called owners in perpetuity, do not hesitate in announcing to the rest of the world and that too at the top of their voices about the theoretical equality that they claim to deliver to the woman. And this they do without any shame or remorse, whatsoever.

Most of the people in this world have fixed ideas and beliefs about everything, including cultures, habits, and lifestyles. In formulating these social behaviors and attitudes, including the fundamental relationship between man and woman, human beings always look to their faiths and allow the religions to play a very crucial role. While many religions of the world seem to encourage equality between the sexes to a certain level, in reality a wide gap persists between what is preached by a religion and what is actually practiced by its followers. Whether a religion has a Western or Eastern origin, it seems not to promote full justice to the cause of woman.

It is not surprising then that one of the most widely accepted and dominant religions puts man on a higher plane than woman. It states that God made man in his own image while woman was a subsequent and secondary creation.[2] Different cultures of the world, likewise, also tend to follow the same pattern more or less. Regardless of what language we might speak, traditional cultures always seem to favor male dominance. In his book on sociology, Ian Robertson appropriately notes that we usually speak of 'man' and 'mankind' when we really mean 'human beings' and 'humanity.[3] Interestingly, the English language, despite being the most commonly-used language of the world, does not have the neuter gender and thus does not have a pronoun to cover cases of 'he or she.' As a result, we generally end up using 'he' when referring to someone whose sex is not

139

specified.[4]

The followers of the Eastern faiths are not far behind in their attitudes towards women. Even in faiths where religious dictums clearly support equality for woman, the followers tend to manipulate these teachings in order to negate the core philosophy of a given faith. Baba Nanak, the founder of the Sikh faith spoke about the status of women in the early 16th century *"So kiuen mandaa aakhiaye, Jitt jumai Rajaan,"*[5] meaning, "How could those, who give birth to emperors and kings be ever called inferior?" He openly announced this at a time when such statements were taboos under the then Mogul rule. But now, it is the people in the home state of Baba Nanak who, more than others, are plainly trying to ignore his teachings. Rather, they all seem hell bent to practice this evil in total contradiction to these well-defined, golden dictums. To a large extent, such pronouncements from Holy Scripture nowadays are kept reserved only for religious sermons on Sundays.

A depressive death-like environment still becomes all too obvious when news arrives about the birth of a female child. Tears (*Aansoos*) flow down continuously in those downcast eyes of the new mother of a female child as she waits in fear to hear the onslaught of rebukes from her husband and mother-in-law. If feticide did not work or was not considered and infanticide is ruled out, then there is a stark possibility that these unwanted female toddlers may become cheap commodities, available for sale especially amongst the exploited weaker and poorer segments of Indian society. It is no secret that some are condemned to a life full of misery and anguish that is no less than a living hell on earth.

Who will ever forget that heart-rending poem by Sahir Ludhianvi, written about half a century ago? *"Aurat ne janum deeyaa mardon ko, Mardon ne usai bazaar deeyaa, Jub jee chaaha kuchla masla, Jub jee chaaha dutkaar deeyaa,"*[6] that means, "The female gives birth to a man, the man sells her like a commodity. At his whim, she could be suppressed, trampled upon and at his whim she could be rebuked and thrown away."

Yet India is a land of contrasts, and its cultural landscape keeps on changing rapidly. The attitudes of the educated urban men in larger cities seem to be undergoing a rapid metamorphosis. India today certainly seems far ahead of much of the developing world in its political awareness about the 'Fair Sex.' The women of India have been enjoying political power much more and much earlier than the so-called 'developed nations' of the West. One of the largest democracies of the world, India elected its first woman Prime Minister close to 40 years ago, at a time when many countries of the world even didn't comprehend the true meaning of the world 'democracy.' Recently a woman was elected in India to the top 'Royal' position as the President of India.

Agreeably, improvement has not reached measurable proportions at all levels of society. And there is lot that needs to be done on the social-cultural front. One would hope that with the rapid revolution in information technology, the day may soon come when the women of India will have access to their long overdue share of safety and survival like their male counterparts.

To end this painful topic in a lighter mode, I have a humble suggestion to make to the Indian confectioners. We all know that *Laddoos* (rounded yellow-colored coarse granular sweet balls, smaller than a tennis ball and very popular in India) are usually distributed by many families in India to their friends and relatives at the birth of a son. It is the Indian confectioners who end up preparing and then selling them to such families. Here is a golden opportunity for the government to promote the equality while allowing the confectioners of the *Laddoos* to double their sales. The government or rather the social

141

philanthropic organizations involved in the welfare of women should subsidize the confectioners so that they could, in turn, give away these *Laddoos* for free to the mothers who deliver female babies. This way the births of newborn baby girls will also be celebrated with the same gusto and sweetness that shows up all around with the distribution of the *Laddoos* at births of male babies. This strategy of giving away of *Laddoos* for free might simply do the trick where strict laws and religious sermons have thus far failed.

Reference: (1, 2, 3, 4) Ian Robertson, Text book of Sociology: Worth Publishers (1987)

      (5) Guru Nanak, Sri Guru Granth Sahib Ji

      (6) Sahir Ludhianvi, in the Movie 'Sadhna'

21.
Old Wines in New Bottles

With the gradual advancement in the economic affluence of the diaspora, the attitudes of its members towards life have also changed. Some unnecessary and redundant customs and traditions from back home that were initially discarded have started to creep back once again into their lives. They seem determined to regain and retain what they saw as lost grounds in early part of their settlements, especially in relation to these customs and traditions. This shift in their behavior is becoming more and more obvious during important celebrations such as marriages, anniversaries, and birthdays of their loved ones.

In fact, the wedding celebrations of the children of the diaspora, being the most joyful for the parents, are the ones most affected with such changes. Given the resources, immigrant parents usually try to show off their richness to the other community members by highlighting their status, culture and material worth. In a sense, it is only through such actions that they can fulfill their fantasies, fantasies that had been 'on hold' for a while.

Gone are the days when the numbers of diaspora members were small and there were few occasions to celebrate. The 25th or 50th wedding anniversaries that are often celebrated nowadays were not on the horizon in the past. Likewise eligible young men and women of marriageable age were limited. And even if weddings did take place, the lack of resources kept such celebrations less elaborate. The elements that made an event a topmost Indian-style celebration -- like highly-trained caterers serving high quality ethnic food, and ethnic decorations in the banquet halls -- were yet not in vogue.

The dreams were out there, but to act upon those dreams was not possible. Once in a while, some of the members of the diaspora, especially those in the bigger cities, were able to recreate the dream celebrations in the back home styles, but such situations were few and far between. The occasional successful duplication of those events often turned them into the 'talk of the town' while others simply considered them another 'show of wealth.' Yet for many ordinary immigrants, a simple marriage ceremony for their offspring was all that was possible, given their financial resources.

With the increase in the numbers of the diaspora members and with the advancement in their riches, such occasions did not stay within the domain of only a few families anymore. Almost anyone who could afford and wished to have the most elaborate 'Regal Style Indian' celebration could turn such dreams into reality without much of a hassle. So far so good! But along with economic affluence, certain socially degrading customs imported from home also started sprouting up, much like unwanted mushrooms in the rainy season.

The dowry, given to daughters at the time of their weddings, was one of the worst customs prevalent among the people of Indian subcontinent. The members of the Indian diaspora have unfortunately started importing and re-introducing that evil once again. In view of the easy affordability and availability of the things-material in these foreign lands, the members of our communities have started to dignify the dowry at a larger and rather sophisticated scale. It is not perceived to be the same kind of curse any more as they saw it while they were in India. It is also believed, albeit erroneously, that the bigger the dowry, longer the marriage will last and the happier will be the days ahead for the newlyweds. However, little do the members of the diaspora realize that such excessive giving, far more than could be considered reasonable, is simply a manifestation of age-old conditioning of the minds? Unfortunately, other than upholding a tradition, it serves no useful purpose. In fact, it often turns interfamily relationships into source of discord that lingers in perpetuity, with no end in sight.

It is becoming more and more apparent that what is being given by the parents of the bride at the time of a wedding in these lands of plenty is often not ordinary. I know of situations where the father of the bride has given the bridegroom the keys of an expensive new automobile like a Cadillac, a Mercedes or even more expensive vehicle. If this were not enough, brides' parents have offered new houses and many other expensive items as part of their daughters' dowries. One might say, "So what? Have not the super-rich NRIs settled in Europe treated their daughters and sons-in-laws with the most expensive gifts on the face of this earth? And have not kings and queens of the past blessed their new sons-in-law with boroughs, counties, and other properties? What is then wrong with giving a car or even several cars in a dowry, so long as the giver can afford it and voluntarily hands it over?"

The question here is not 'giving' in itself. If one can afford it and wishes to give it, let it be so. But when one tries to make large gifts an essential component of the marriage ceremony, as it is in India, it assumes another kind of significance. Such giving obviously represents a 'dowry,' with all of its unfortunate consequences, regardless of the fact that it might come wrapped in the best of intentions. This is not 'giving' in the true sense of the word.

Moreover, the diaspora recipients of dowries in Western countries often have no true need for such items. In fact, they end up expecting such expensive gifts as a matter of their rights, even if the intent of giving is different in the minds of the givers. There is a perception that some dowry-seeking parents of bridegrooms in the West have also started pressuring parents of the brides for excessive gifts, directly or indirectly. The unfortunate parents of the brides find themselves in a bind while trying their best to fulfill the demands posted by the bridegroom's family. At times, they end up borrowing or spending their lifesavings to please their daughter's future in-laws.

This establishes a bad precedent for all those who have marriageable daughters waiting at their doorsteps, but may not be able to support such extravagant gifts in a dowry. When one starts raising the bar of expectations of future sons-in-law about the possibility of expensive dowry gifts, it certainly enhances their market value in their own eyes. The men then refuse to set their feet on ground. One might say that girls are free to find the husbands of their choices, but in practical terms many marriages among the diaspora still take place with the blessings of the parents on both sides of the aisle.

The menace that dowries represent in India is well-known to all. The frequent suicides by young brides as a consequence of their inability to bring expensive gifts for their in-laws are not lost on any of us. Likewise, the tortures given to new brides by their in-laws, including homicides, for their failure to fulfill the in-laws' ever-expanding demands are everyday phenomenon in the news media. Admittedly, the new bride in the Western world might not take such an extreme action of killing herself. She also might not let her in-laws inflict any bodily harm upon her. Still, the emotional trauma cannot be entirely avoided. Such emotional torture and blackmail can lead to divorce, and I have no doubt that one could find an abundance of such examples among the daughters of the diaspora members.

There is another reality of Western culture that one usually does not talk about but which cannot be ignored. Many marriages here do not last unto death, regardless of what one might wish. Why, then, is there such a need for handing over expensive gifts to someone who might not even continue his relationship with the daughter of the giver? In such a scenario, expensive gifts may simply act like oil on the fire and further complicate matters. Such gifts become the source of ongoing legal battles and lead to painful and irreparable divisiveness in relationships that end up in divorce.

My intent here is not directed against gift-giving per se. There will be plenty of occasions in the future for those who wish to bless their daughters and sons-in-law when their married lives become more settled, stronger and grandchildren begin arriving on the scene. Being a grandparent is a great excuse for giving!

I am also not preaching against helping newlywed couples who often need some financial assistance in establishing themselves in the earlier stages of their marriage. A helping hand from the parents can do much for a young couple. But giving only for the purpose of showing off just to fulfill an obsolete custom of offering a dowry has its own adverse repercussions. The custom of dowry with its origin mired into ill-founded concepts and the one with unfortunate consequences, more than what meets the eyes, needs to be avoided, at least among the people who are settled in the West. Nothing is wrong with letting go off those cultural artifacts that are harmful while retaining traditions that truly benefit us and our future generations.

22.

Architectural Treasures of India Are Fading into Ruins: Does Anyone Care?

India happens to be one of the richest countries in the world when it comes to its history and unique architecture of the times past, including forts, palaces, and historical religious sites. Its legendary emperors, kings, and navaabs dedicated their lives and poured their blood to creating extraordinary pieces of imagination and art. But the precious treasures of unique architecture are now slowly but steadily slipping away from us, fading, thanks to the negligence of those who were and are supposed to be their protectors. The true value and significance of these possessions have always eluded us, the inheritors of these gems. My visit to the town of Jaipur in Rajasthan, India, a few years ago brought this painful reality back to me and compelled me to share my thoughts with my fellow members of the diaspora.

Why is it that despite inheriting the most unusual and extraordinarily sophisticated historical treasures, like none others in the world, have we turned a blind eye to their maintenance? Why is it that even modern buildings of great architectural value, some built since partition of India, have become so dilapidated as to make one cry? Why is it that despite having the largest labor pool in the world, those responsible for maintaining these precious jewels seem not to care for their jobs? Why is it that these buildings never get repaired or only get repaired when a visit from a high level Union Minister or President of the country is due? Once the paint fades away on these buildings or the concrete starts chipping, everyone ignores as if it were an old, dying, helpless and homeless person on its last breath that is of no concern to anyone. Why is it that world-class palaces, long praised for their beauty, are being allowed to turn into heaps of debris? And why is it that the pigeon droppings have become more prominent than the paint that was supposed to grace these buildings?

Why is it that people from all over the world come to marvel at the architectural supremacy of our country, but end up looking at the mounds of rubble instead? And why is it that the roads leading to these exotic pieces of art are allowed to be occupied by unfortunate homeless transients who are considered and treated no better than garbage by our politicians? Where are those so-called special heritage cells and departments that are supposed to look after our precious heritage? Are they to exist only on paper?

The historical buildings or governmental properties are not the only ones that are facing this dilemma. The situation of the religious sites of yesterday, with their extraordinary historical and spiritual significance, is no different. They seem to be suffering the same fate despite the amount of income they generate through donations, income that literally shames the collections of the state governments in which they are located. Instead of maintaining them in conditions that bring comfort to the eyes and solace to the minds, they are allowed to disintegrate and oftentimes voluntarily torn apart into pieces in the name of expansion and modernization. It makes one wonder why the leaders of these historical religious shrines consider their maintenance a fruitless and unnecessary effort?

Why is it that after a road is built in India, it is expected to last forever without any repairs regardless of number of potholes and people who use it? Why is it that so many people end up dying on the roads due to poor maintenance, and yet nobody makes a noise to correct the problem? As with much else in India, there are lots of questions but no answers. Talk to any Indian here or back home and a ready-made response will strike your ears, "Nothing can be done in India due to rampant and pervasive corruption." End of the story. This is mostly true, but looking at this issue a little bit more critically, one realizes that this may not be so.

The world we live in has become much smaller with the rapid advent and progress in the field of information technology, the Internet, television and other media. The ease of international travel keeps on inspiring people from all over the world to come to India to visit its architectural marvels and learn more about the glorious past of the country. In order to facilitate and further promote tourism from other countries, the improvement and upkeep of places of historical interest should have been at the top of India's agenda. Those at the helm of affairs should have made it their business to keep these historical priceless gems in top notch conditions. It would not only have brought positive attention but also much needed dollars and cents for upkeep.

In order to achieve such objectives, the government should have followed the examples of the Western world. Each and every point of interest in the Western world, even in the richest countries, whether historical or otherwise, charges an admission fee for an entry. The revenue collected from visitors is spent on maintenance and upgrades of the facilities.

Unfortunately, this kind of concept has remained alien to our culture for reasons that don't make any sense. However, recently this Western-style approach to the management of national treasures may be gaining some ground within the Indian consciousness. But as always, it is too late and too little. One only hopes that with passage of time, this change in thought process will keep on making further inroads, for there is nothing wrong to ask visitors to pay for the pleasure of enjoying such monuments of rare beauty but at a level field, irrespective of the country of origin.

It remains to be seen, however, if revenues thus collected will actually be spent on the crumbling pieces of architecture in dire need of repair. Or if the money will slip into the pockets of unscrupulous politicians, middlemen and contractors soaked in corruption, leaving maintenance in an unfinished state. I hope and pray that such will never be the case.

There is another aspect to the poor upkeep of historical buildings that needs consideration here. The concept of not paying due attention to maintenance and the disdain for blue collar physical work, even in one's own household, is deeply rooted in the Indian mind and is often left for domestic servants. This is totally contrary to the culture of the Western world, where the dignity of labor for personal and other needs is not considered shameful at all. To further elaborate this point, one only needs to remember the example set by the daughter of one of the American presidents in the recent past who did not hesitate to babysit at the White House in order to make little extra money beyond her weekly allowance. Her duty included changing diapers of the toddlers for whom she was caring.

Can one ever imagine such a down-to-earth attitude from an ordinary teenager in India, not to mention children of our well-placed leaders? Presidents Carter and Clinton could have easily afforded a coolie – or even a Marine colonel -- to carry their bags, but they saw a certain amount of dignity in carrying their personal briefcases themselves. Can one ever imagine a politician in India, even a low level one, showing such an attitude about carrying his or her own bag?

It is difficult to change the attitudes of the billion-plus people of India, attitudes that have been ingrained over many generations. I also know that the corruption that has become part of daily life is not going to go away anytime soon. But if during our visits, we could bring this point home to our relatives and friends, implore them through personal as well as practical examples, and motivate them to get involved, it might eventually have an impact, someday, somewhere. At least one purpose of our leaving home and settling into the Western world should have been to pick up what is good here and transport such ideas back to those whom we left behind.

Our historical architectural treasures deserve a chance to survive. They were created by their builders to please the eyes of many future generations. But they can only achieve that purpose if they are kept in their original condition and not be allowed to crumble and vanish away from the face of the earth. If we don't take steps quickly to undo the harm that is being inflicted upon our natural and architectural treasures through our negligence, then God bless them and us.

Our lack of respect for physical labor and our failure to institute methods to replenish these dwindling resources will ultimately expedite the demise of these priceless jewels. If we fail to act, they will be gone forever. And if that were to happen, our motherland and our ancestors will never forgive us. And then it may be too late. Does anyone care to listen?

SQUARE PEGS, ROUND HOLES

23.
India! Sweet India! Here We Come!

The members of the Indian diaspora often get opportunities to go back to their mother countries for visits. The people traveling to India from Canada or the U.S. usually have to stop somewhere in Europe if traveling eastward via the Atlantic. Planes stop in Singapore, Seoul, Hong Kong, Tokyo or Malaysia if the flights are westward across the Pacific Ocean. In the first leg of the eastward flights, the passengers usually represent a mix of people from the Western world. Flights across the Pacific, on the other hand, often carry Asians whose ethnicity is dependent upon the countries that fall en route. After the stop and before the flight starts on its second leg, the plane is thoroughly and totally cleaned, as expected.

Once the plane takes off for India again, the dynamic as well as the culture within the plane changes abruptly. The majority of the passengers on the second leg of the flight to India are often Indians, and it is this part of the flight to which I wish to draw attention. The peculiarities, behaviors, and characteristics of the passengers change dramatically, setting us, the Indians, apart from the rest. The attitude of the crew also changes, perhaps as a result of the metamorphosis of the passengers' ethnicity.

As soon as the pilot allows the passengers to remove their seatbelts, it seems like a hurricane has suddenly moved through the plane's cabin, causing huge disarray. It only proves that we might have been living in Western countries for a long time, but when it comes to creating a mess, we seem not to forget our culture, good or not -so-good. We show our real selves by the mayhem we create inside the plane. Our style of chatter, our clumsy use of the plane's bathrooms, and the incessant flurry of demands put upon the hostesses, all add up to that well-known chaotic scene.

The freedom we give to our tag-along children in allowing them to do whatever they wish during the flight is beyond description. We do not seem to mind their running up and down in the aisles or their incessant need to go to bathrooms, because for us they are still poor little babies. Rather, through our actions, we proudly try to inform the rest of the world that being Indians, we are family-oriented. That is why irrespective of their age, we wish to take our children home to visit their grandparents and other close relatives so that they could stay in touch with their extended families. Of course, there is nothing wrong with taking young children back to our motherland, as it keeps the little ones in touch with their heritage. But avoiding our responsibility in guiding them to act responsibly adds to the mayhem, especially when the discipline for Indian children has always been in short supply to begin with.

As the flight progresses, we become acutely aware of

impending tiredness. We do not wish to feel exhausted upon arrival back to the country of our birth, so we try to take a nap en route, even if it requires dozing off or snoring loudly on the shoulder of the poor passenger sitting in the next seat. And this is bound to happen, for we just finished our hearty meals provided by our favorite airline. God save the fellow passengers from our loud belches thereafter! Still we always have reasons to justify our attitudes by pretending that it is not our problem. When sleep finally overpowers us, we remind ourselves to cover our heads and eyes; we must avoid all outside contact to get into a deeper slumber.

At the same time, we expect the crew to keep on serving us every time and all the times we call them. And don't we also want the crew to be aware that we, the Indians, are mostly vegetarians? The food must be of our choice and our liking, for after all, we are coming from 'phorren'. Fortunately, in order to stay competitive, most of the airlines flying to India nowadays have taken steps to provide Indian food, especially Indian vegetarian food. And why not? After all we, the Indians, pay for our tickets like everyone else.

We also want to make sure that we have a truckload of gifts for all of our relatives, without regard to the airlines' limits on weights or sizes of the suitcases. And if they get overloaded, the Indian wives are always ready to oblige their husbands by taking a bigger purse. If that doesn't work, we can always order them to take an even bigger one or hide a second one under their clothing. We somehow try to justify by reminding our wives that it's a matter of only a few hours of discomfort. We also convince ourselves that we will find a way to get onto the planes with all our bags and belongings, hoping that the crew will understand our unique situation. After all, we are not only looking after the needs of our little children while on a visit, but also the needs of a truckloads of relatives waiting to be obliged as soon as we land.

Once the pilot announces that we are about to land in India, it does not take us long to run up to the front door, crushing all those who are not quick enough to compete. It is not our fault if they cannot walk fast enough. We have to let the world know through our unique attitudes, actions and behaviors that we still remain the same old Indians at hearts!

Most of the landings in India are at midnight when our minds and bodies are half asleep, having been en route for over 24 hours without any shower or personal cleansing. That peculiar fragrance, a combination of tropical air coupled with humidity emanating from the motherland, awaits us eagerly to welcome our nostrils. This immediately seems to bring back bundles of those forgotten memories, both good and not-so-good.

The continuous shrills of little children don't help either but rather add to the strange welcome or, rather, the un-welcoming reception we receive from the snobbish customs officials. In the past, the customs officials at Indian international airports would often give a hard time to passengers, especially those who carried more gifts than the law allowed. In order to get around this dilemma, some passengers made the customs officials happy by parting with some of their hard-earned dollars, or a few of the gifts that originally were brought for members of their extended families.

To avoid getting caught, some ingenious passengers would wear several layers of socks, sweaters, turbans, and jackets, one on top of the other, never mention the heat and humidity outside. Who doesn't remember those times when serious attempts were made to hide the accompanying loads of electronic gifts, here and there, praying the whole trip for divine intervention that the customs officials would not find all that was being brought in? Thanks to Prime Minister S. Manmohan Singh, procedures at the airports have gotten better, and some semblance of Western-style normalcy has taken place.

The pale-looking customs officials with sunken cheeks, more than half-covered with thick glasses, stand ready to confront the dead-tired travelers who are neither asleep nor awake. The officials keep on trying their best to balance those thick glasses on the rather thin bridges of their noses. But alas! The weight of the heavy glasses refuses to cooperate. As such, the spectacles keep sliding down to the tips of their noses, preventing the customs officials from making direct eye contact with semi-asleep and the weary passengers. The complete apathy of these officials ultimately becomes fully obvious when they straighten their necks in an attempt to look at the passengers. The queer frowns on their foreheads seem to question the very right of the people to visit their birth country. Documents are inspected at a slow tortoise pace. Their sarcastic attitudes and behaviors often lead to horrendous delays in clearing the poor passengers' documents.

Reluctantly stamping the passport with a loud thump, the customs officials project an impression that the passengers have committed a grave crime by returning to their motherland. If this wasn't enough, the passengers are made to feel that now when they have finally arrived, they are at the total mercy of these bosses of the day who are doing a great favor by letting the passengers in. Moreover through their attitudes, these customs officials try to subtly let the passengers know that somehow it was their fault that the customs officials could not have an opportunity to leave India for foreign lands, like the passengers did.

On the other hand, the passengers are no saints either. Oftentimes, some of them have pre-arranged with airport officials to get ahead of the line, ignoring the frowns on the foreheads as well as the helpless expressions on the faces of the others waiting in-line ahead of them. After all, we care for rules and regulations only when we are out of India. "Anything goes in India!" is the mantra by which we, the

Indians, try to defend ourselves against the uneasiness that may creep in our minds whenever we break the rules.

But the problems and issues of visits back home do not end here. As soon as one finally gets an opportunity to liberate oneself from the clutches of the immigration officials, an army of taxi drivers and coolies appear at the curb of the airport wooing the passengers to use their services. Likewise, many other not-so-needed advisors for a myriad of unsolicited services begin bothering the exhausted travelers incessantly and in full force, so much so that it truly becomes very difficult to get rid of them without being taken in. One has to fight one's way to ultimately reach the welcoming embrace of those relatives who have traveled long distances the night before, spending big time in travel. At times, they suffer much more discomfort than the passenger itself and may have to wait in long lines just to meet and greet the travelers.

And thus begins the onward journey back to our home town leading to another story to be told at a different time.

24.
About Discipline and Our People

Of all the people whom God Almighty created and who ever walked on the face of this earth we, the people of India, happen to possess some unique characteristics. This statement is based upon the prevalence of certain special attributes and behaviors among us, both good and not so good. Some among us consider these special characteristics as assets, while others might simply presume them to be liabilities. In this article, I would like to highlight one of these behaviors that relates to our well-known lack of discipline, at least among some of us. My intent here is simply to highlight what I have observed, experienced and read. Fortunately, it is not true for all and thus no pun is intended.

Lack of discipline is one deficiency that we, the Indians, could have certainly done without. Instead, it seems to totally plague many of us from top to the bottom and from inside out. Having assumed a kind of special notoriety in almost all angles of our lifestyles in India, it now seems to be disseminating wherever Indians happen to emigrate. Interestingly, we have accepted it so much that we consider this lack of discipline to be synonymous with being what we are. It often makes me wonder if God Almighty ran short of the discipline ingredient precisely when it was time to make the recipe of our people.

This lack of discipline among Indians is quite obvious, regardless of the status of the person or the situation. Starting from the top elected body in India, i.e. the Indian Parliament, down to the level of small family gatherings, the same pattern repeats itself. An absence of discipline is everywhere. In fact this lack of discipline happens to be the root cause of many problems that we, as a nation, have faced for centuries and are confronting yet today.

We often hear, read or see the news about the functioning of India's parliament and its state-level legislative bodies. The people of India elect their representatives to govern their country and states. Once elected, these representatives consider their elected status as a 'blank check' for causing mayhem in those august bodies. Their jobs were to frame the laws in a civilized manner and within a common set of protocols for the benefit and governance of their constituents. Rather, they become determined to disrupt the very functioning of the institutions i.e. the parliament and legislative bodies, where such laws were to be framed.

One would have hoped that with the passage of time our democratic thinking and working might have matured. Many citizens believe that our elected representatives eventually will learn something from the established democracies of the West. But the situation seems to be worsening day by day, session by session, and now the phenomenon seems to have totally gotten out of hand. It is present all the time, every time, whenever these legislative bodies meet. In fact this behavior has become the norm rather than the exception.

This lack of discipline among us becomes more obvious during our travels on the streets and roads of India. Respect for traffic signs and the "rules of the road" are not in our blood. Rather, we are much better at shedding blood on these highways and by-ways. We accept the eventuality of accidents causing injuries and deaths as the 'Will of God' and a simple fact of life. Carelessness and negligence are the hallmarks of our lifestyle in India. Common sense dictates that after constant suffering from the consequences of lawlessness, the people should have become more careful, but that isn't case. Rather, our tendency to ignore discipline continues to persist.

The aversion to discipline persists even after we have decided to emigrate and settle permanently in other countries. Even at our religious institutions, where we gather the most on the weekends and on special occasions, the practice of discipline is often not on our agenda. Being a Sikh, I can and will limit my discomfort and criticisms to my personal experiences at Sikh religious institutions. Still, it should surprise no one in finding similar patterns of behavior at other Eastern religious places.

Religious functions in most of our religious institutions in the West, like Christian churches and Jewish synagogues, usually begin at 10 a.m. rather than during the early ambrosial hours. On top of it, the services take place only once a week on Sundays as if the court of God only opens for business one day a week. And yet only a handful of devotees show up on time. The majority will start arriving at noon in a laid-back, leisurely fashion, coincidently just before the start of the free kitchen or *Lungar*. The late arrivals rarely seem concerned about the disturbances they cause in the congregation by their arrivals in the middle of services.

The primary purpose for attending religious services is usually to listen, to learn, to understand and then to follow what is preached there. But those who have ever visited our religious places will agree with me that this is the last thing we do. Constant background chatter, especially among the elderly ladies, happens to be a regular feature of our services. It is as if somebody had just let them loose after holding them in solitary confinement and they now have this rare opportunity to meet and greet their long separated friends and relatives. All of their pent-up issues and gossips have to be released at that very moment. Caring for what goes on in the service seems to be the least of their concerns. From their behaviors, they obviously think that the house of God belongs to them, at least as much as, if not more than it belongs to the ones who are performing religious services on the podium. How could another mortal, even if that happens to be a professional religious person, dare stop them from carrying on the chatter that they wish to continue?

Now compare this to a service in a church or synagogue where all must take their seats before the service begins. The services usually start right on time with everyone paying full attention, quietly, without children running around and without that background chatter. The attendees know that they have come to the church or synagogue for a specific purpose of joining in the service and not to exchange gossip or settle their personal scores. There is no discussion of personal issues and no wasting of time through socialization during the services.

The crude management of our religious places, under the garb of democracy, allows the managers and organizers to create a mess where there should be none. Frequent internal bickering and arguments over holding onto offices keeps the flame of discontent burning, erupting into violence at times. The religious institutions that are supposed to provide peace and solace to the spiritually-deprived and allegedly-Westernized Indians often turn into battlegrounds, thanks to this lack of the discipline. The ego-driven managers try to keep the religiously-oriented and apolitical souls away from jumping into the fray to sort the matters out. Despite their desire to make mend, such spiritually oriented individuals end up turning into mere spectators.

After having lived in Western countries among people with a fair degree of respect for discipline, one would think that we might have learned a lesson or two, but this isn't the case. In fact, it is shameful to say that this disease of undisciplined behavior in our religious places is much more prevalent among expatriates than it is among those remaining in our native land. Might it be that having come from India, the so-called epicenter of spirituality, we try to act as if God is in our grip and that we are free to do whatever we wish in our religious places?

Our penchant for arriving late, sometimes very late, is not limited to religious functions. It has been so deeply ingrained in our psyche that Indian functions can be defined as 'undisciplined functions featuring the late arrival of the guests.' We try to rationalize that everybody else will be late anyway, so why should it matter if we are late as well? By contrast, when it comes to forming queues for getting onto buses and trains or whatever else, the tendency amongst Indians is one of hurriedness and 'me first.' We simply forget the practice of patience, thinking that such concerns are of no matter to us. This behavior, at times, also comes to the fore when watching an Indian waiting for an elevator. The time-honored practice of letting those inside make their exit before we rush in is usually ignored.

One could argue that many of our behaviors and characteristics are simply the consequence of back home habits and therefore destined to stay with us for as long as we live. In this equation it is conveniently forgotten that since the events of 9-11, the ground rules have drastically

165

changed. Life is much more difficult for people who do not fit the usual cultural profiles of Tom, Dick and Harry. It is becoming more and more obvious that as practitioners of less-than culturally-acceptable habits in this culture, we will be facing more challenges in the long run. It is here that we need to rise to the occasion, become watchful, and work hard to unlearn habits that could inadvertently provide opportunities for others to criticize and take a jibe at us for no faults of our own other than our just appearing different.

25.

Indian Children Growing up in the West in the Presence of Grandparents

Every Sunday while attending services at a local Gurdwara, I watch parents holding the hands of their little children and guiding them to bow in front of Guru Granth Sahib Ji with humility, reverence and discipline before they take their seats. Once in a while, one gets to experience the reverse. Some elders from India using canes or walkers and in need of help are guided by their little American-born grandchildren. These children are not yet fully mature, but despite their young ages, they seem to fully enjoy their assigned responsibilities. They try their best to exhibit concern and ensure that their brittle, elderly grandparents are not pushed or pulled excessively. These little angels try to walk and bow like adults and exhibit a fair degree of maturity despite their tender ages. They stay with their grandparents throughout the services and seem not to care, even if they miss their activities with other children of their age.

Most of them are born and raised in the West by immigrant parents and go to the same schools as the children of indigenous Americans. But when it comes to awareness about the well-being of their parents and grandparents, the differences becomes obvious. In fact, this difference is what made me think and write about this piece.

The lifestyle of Indians in India as well as in the countries abroad is rapidly changing, thanks to the strong influence of Western culture. The Western culture's affinity for emphasizing an attitude of 'me first, me only, and me all' is truly like a magnet, attracting everyone. Added to the 'me first' attitude is the emphasis on youth and youthfulness. Everyone agrees that many cultural and economical aspects of the lifestyles in the Western world, to say the least, are impeccable. If it were not so, many of us would not have come here. Yet, what is bothersome is the continuous erosion of some of the worthy characteristics and qualities that we brought with us from back home.

One of the major qualities of Eastern culture that has been passed down from generation to generation is the commitment to take care of the elderly, especially parents and grandparents. Slowly and steadily, after settling in the West, the immigrants from the countries of the East start to lose this noble cultural concept in their rather hurried steps towards a superficial assimilation. Our children learn their behaviors from what they watch and absorb from the surroundings in which they live. The centuries-old practice of India's extended-family system that offers a respectable and active status to the grandparents in family matters has always created a positive impact on many growing children in India. It exposes Indian children to a practical way of taking care of the grandparents. The grandparents, on the other hand, enjoy having a say in the household regarding the growth and development of their grandchildren.

After immigrating to the West, the young parents of these little children first have to establish themselves and this requires a lot of time and efforts. In order to make a reasonable living and achieve a comfortable lifestyle, both parents end up working. Not only do they have to work hard, but they also must endure longer hours of absence from home and children. In such an environment, the first casualty happens to be the children who are left home alone or those who have to be outsourced to a babysitter. In situations where children are not under the direct observation of a close and reliable relative, problems tend to ensue. Young children need social interaction and guidance. When these are in short supply, any resulting developmental or emotional damage, though not apparent, may end up sustaining its ill-effects for the rest of their lives. Having grandparents around not only serves the intended purpose of babysitting but it also brings a sense of closeness to these children. The love and affection that grandparents shower on young children is much more than anything money can ever buy.

Additionally, the presence of the grandparents makes these young children develop the skills to communicate with them easily in their language and thus learn and develop those well-established Eastern moral values. The grandparents also find it easier to share their thoughts with their grandchildren, thus allowing the children of newer generations to remain connected to their roots.

Not all immigrants from India share such a philosophy, and many may question the usefulness of having such close connections with their 'roots.' They may believe that once we are here, we are here forever, and sooner or later our generations will assimilate with the indigenous culture.

So what is the need for putting extraordinary efforts into maintaining those roots? Looking at the Hispanic and other immigrant minorities who preceded us, it becomes apparent that a concept of retaining one's 'roots' is not foolproof, and in a good number of situations, it doesn't happen despite a great amount of effort.

The Western culture and lifestyle often makes family relationships distant and artificial. The eventualities of old age are never explained to the children. Rather, the children born in this culture are actively and intentionally kept away from the sick and invalid. They are denied the opportunity to witness the difficulties of later life, as well as the natural processes of death and dying. The parents find no time to encourage or take their children to religious institutions where discussion and guidance about life and its related difficulties usually take place.

Allowing the children to grow under the umbrella of mature guidance of their grandparents will provide them with the impetus to look beyond this superficial and filtered lifestyle. They will be able to experience the ups and downs in the lives of people in the last years of their stay on the earth. Such experiences will help prepare them for their future encounters with such issues when their own parents turn old and infirm. Becoming part of the lives of elderly grandparents at a time when the minds of children are still in developing stages, can ultimately offer such children a wholesome view of entire span of life. Living with the grandparents will prime them to face the real world, far beyond that which they gain from a lifestyle of instant gratification that is so prevalent all around them, all the time in the Western world.

Ironically, the family values often talked about in Western countries are limited in scope usually to spouses and immediate children. Grandparents – the parents of the parents -- are not included or considered part of the core family, both legally and culturally. In the American culture, an adult often will refer to his or her spouse's parents as "her folks" or "his folks." This clearly speaks volumes about the relationship she or he perceives or the respect she or he has for the parents of each other's spouse. Like many others, I also did not comprehend this phenomenon when I entered this culture in the early seventies for the first time. However, the awakening about this Western cultural novelty, if one may call it so, didn't take long to dawn upon me.

Given the prevalent concept of remoteness and self-indulgence in Western culture, there is a dire need for all of us to take pause. The presence of grandparents during the development of growing children is a blessing we can ill-afford to ignore. Every effort must be made by those whose parents are still alive to arrange for their presence during the growing phase of their own children.

The path shown by this age-old golden concept of Indian culture in offering due respect to the elderly and helpless grandparents will be a blessing for which their children will always be obligated and thankful. In this lies not only a great benefit for our children, but also the Mukti or salvation that we so dearly seek throughout our living days on Mother Earth.

SQUARE PEGS, ROUND HOLES

26.
Conversation Styles of Immigrants

The easy availability of air transportation during the past century has made international travel frequent and within the reach of ordinary people all over the world. Despite such convenience, inter-country migration on a permanent basis was quite limited early on. Perhaps most people didn't feel a need to leave their mother countries and settle abroad permanently. With the passage of time, the economic interdependence among different countries became a reality and the frequency of world travel gradually took a further jump. As a result, the world truly started to shrink for ordinary people. The travel from point A to point B, both in terms of time and resources became easy.

The rich nations kept on adopting new laws and new regulations in order to open the borders of their countries by unlocking their gates. This made it somewhat easier for non-natives to enter via legal channels. They did so primarily for their own economic reasons. But this turned out to be a great boon for under-developed nations with mushrooming populations, nations that were already at their wits end in finding new opportunities for their people.

Most people who emigrated from old world nations had not been able to realize their full potentials in their motherlands. Their home countries lacked the infrastructures and resources necessary for their progress and thus their will and hard work did not find appropriate outlets. Their entry into Western countries changed the equation for them completely. Finding abundant opportunities in their adopted homelands and, especially with their willingness to work in an accelerated mode, the newly arrived immigrants often surpassed natives in economic prosperity. They started blossoming in their chosen professions thanks to the fertile grounds of Western culture. Slowly but surely, the immigrants adopted many of the habits and trappings of Western life. This metamorphosis indeed helped them assimilate into the prevalent new cultures to a great extent.

The English language has been on firm footing for centuries, not only in its native land i.e. the United Kingdom but also in the U. S. and Canada as well as in Australia and other commonwealth nations. English has always served as a major means of communication among people of different ethnicities settled in these countries.

During the latter part of the 20th century, when significant Asian migration started to take place in North America, Great Britain and Australia, English was the only language through which they could have possibly communicated with one another. The majority of migrating people from South Asia, especially those from the Indian subcontinent, arrived with good comprehension and fluency in English which turned out to be a great catalyst. This truly enabled their entry and assimilation into Western countries. In fact, knowledge of English has been one of the principal reasons for the extraordinary success of these immigrants in the foreign lands. Still notwithstanding their fluency in English, sometimes immigrants have difficulty in mastering the local vernacular, a fact that sets them apart from natives.

New arrivals from foreign lands naturally import the baggage of their own cultures, including dress styles, food habits and languages. In the West, native populations initially tolerated such aberrations simply for their exotic tinge. As time passed, acceptance of foreigners became somewhat less universal. Frowns on the foreheads of natives became commonplace in the presence of immigrants as the unique lifestyles of the latter seemed to define them as 'outsiders.' It was becoming fairly obvious that all was not well on the Western front. Incompatibility, especially in relation to the conversation patterns, finally started showing its true color. It highlighted the differences between the so-called 'foreign born' and the 'native born.'

While exotic foreign foods often received a respectable welcome at the taste buds of the host country natives, conversation patterns, the most important component of 'things-foreign' took the strongest hit. In a way this was bound to happen. Traditionally, the language of the majority – the vernacular, always maintains an upper hand in a multi-ethnic society. It always forms the basis for all communications, without regard to the limited language skills of non-native minority groups.

Conversation, irrespective of one's background, is the most significant vehicle of interaction with our fellow human beings. Therefore, one always hoped that the immigrants would naturally use all the available opportunities and means to sharpen their skills in the language that was prevalent among the majority for the communications. Yet outside of the presence of natives, non-native members of society are often noted to revert back to the comfort and ease of their own languages, thus slowing their development and integration into the mainstream of the society.

No doubt while one always feels most comfortable when communicating through one's mother tongue, it only makes sense that what is being spoken must be understood by all concerned. Moreover, conversations need not turn into shouting matches among immigrants that could effectively exclude all natives. I mentioned here shouting matches because loud, unabated conversations have been noted to be fairly common among many non-native groups in the U.S., especially Asians and Latinos. There is nothing illegal or wrong with such conversations if all the parties to the conversation do not object. However, when such habitual and loud use of the vocal cords takes place in one's own language in the presence of natives who cannot understand the foreign language, it certainly is a cause for concern. It makes them perplexed and with time such behavior induces annoyance and may even breed hatred in the minds of natives.

Speaking aloud in one's native language in the workplace where the majority doesn't understand the ethnic language can end up making colleagues suspicious, putting the speaker at a disadvantage. Loud personal calls in the mother tongue, at the top of one's voice, in the presence of colleagues at work not familiar with the language, is also a poor etiquette.

Likewise, loud conversations in an ethnic language by a visiting relative or a friend at the bedside of a sick ethnic patient in the hospital is disgraceful behavior, especially when done in the presence of another patient lying in the adjoining bed, unfamiliar with the language being spoken. Not only does it create a nuisance, it increases the misery of people who are already ill. Yet all too often, we tend not to care and simply ignore the limits defined by courtesy and good manners.

At this point, I must make it clear that there are times when it is impossible to avoid such situations. However, every attempt must be made to make such conversations tolerable for English-only natives. Bringing the volume down to a lower, softer and gentler tone is always appreciated, as is providing a concurrent translation in English when needed and deemed appropriate.

In democratic and free countries like the U.S., we have the freedom to do what we wish to do and speak what we wish to speak, but it has to be done within the boundaries of the law. Common sense demands reasonable limits. In a multi-ethnic society such as of the U.S., one of the most fundamental etiquettes that needs to be kept in mind is to behave in a way that doesn't interfere with the sensitivities of others. Simply stated, ignoring the presence of others who do not understand our conversation is an insult to those so excluded. Treading on others feet, even unintentionally, should never be attempted, unless we wish the same treatment for ourselves.

27.
Our Rights, Our Responsibilities

Arriving on the shores of a Western country with the intent of making it a permanent abode, many among the new immigrants often feel atop 'cloud nine.' Having lived their lives in countries where material comforts do not match people's rising expectations, the fresh air of the West immediately provides a great respite. Most new immigrants, prior to their arrival, are already familiar with many rights of personal freedom that are available in the West. Yet the responsibilities that also come along with their newfound freedom in their adopted homelands are not so obvious to them.

The transformation from being a member of the majority back home to a distinct and relatively small minority group in a foreign country brings a plethora of its own problems. Initially these problems are blurred and often not clearly visible in the fog of excitement that appears from an abrupt change of culture. In experiencing certain less-than-acceptable situations, it doesn't take long for one to become aware of the fundamental difference between the freedom that one enjoyed as a member of the dominant majority in the birth country compared to the restrictions one now faces as a member of the minority. The reality of one's new life starts hitting home sooner than later. While some individuals belonging to minority groups in their native lands might have some inkling of such differences prior to packing their baggage for this new home, the majority of the immigrants however, are not aware of the changes and for them the transformation turns out to be the real 'cultural shock.'

As a member of a minority, one is often misunderstood, perceived and treated differently from that of the majority, regardless of one's ethnic background and socio-economical status. And this happens to be generally true, irrespective of the country one happens to be living in. I vividly remember that whenever an adverse news about the Sikhs, especially turbaned Sikhs in India, was reported by the news media, the entire Sikh community would be denigrated and blamed for it. It seemed as if each and every member of that minority community, in this case the Sikhs, was responsible for that unbecoming behavior of one individual. Such kinds of examples abound all around us, all over the world.

In a multicultural and multinational society, irrespective of whether it is of the East or West, it is the majority group that more often than not first establishes then applies and interprets the rules of the society. Minority groups end up on the fringes and usually pay the consequences. The immigrants being in minority in the West naturally face the same fate.

Obviously some members of the majority group could never understand the consequences of such an attitude for one has to truly experience it in order to comprehend it. Having said so, it is essential to keep in mind here that this might not have been a manifestation of intentional discrimination on the part of an individual belonging to the majority segment. Rather, it may be a simple outcome of ingrained human nature that all of us happen to possess, more or less.

As a South Asian minority group in this adopted homeland, we need to give some serious thought as to how we used to act in the role of the majority while living back home and how we now try to respond as members of a minority. This should make us more cognizant of the behavioral changes, if any, that we may need to adopt as a consequence of the role reversal that has taken place.

We did import certain attitudes, behaviors and lifestyles from back home. Likewise, the people who have lived in the West for long certainly have their own. There is a need to recognize that some of our previous attitudes might not sit well with the established norms of this country. Unless we, the members of a minority, are willing to make some compromises, there are bound to be under currents of disapproval and resentment.

We have the freedom and the right to own our own residences and businesses, whatever those may be and wherever we choose to locate them. At the same time, we have an unwritten responsibility that our actions should not interfere with the lifestyles of our neighbors or with the established norms of the businesses in which we engage.

There is nothing here that isn't common knowledge. But all too often we, at least some of us, continue to pursue certain habits that are clearly contrary to the customs of the 'natives.'

For example, some of us may fail to maintain the landscaping of our front lawns in good shape, at least on-par with our neighbors. A few among us may try to park our cars in front of others' driveways when attending parties or religious functions at friends' homes. It is not to say that the others do not break the rules but when a member of a small minority violates the customary practices of the overwhelming majority, even in a minor way, that act puts the entire minority group in a negative light. It's unfair, but that's the way it is, the world over.

In regards to business, East Asian motel owners are a case in point. A little laxity, and get ready for all the negative publicity through big headlines in the media that makes their lives tough and ruins their businesses. Likewise, the small corner convenience stores and gas stations, owned by many of our people, have plenty of their own problems. The hard work and long hours these people devote to their businesses definitely makes them tremendously successful in their endeavors. Yet the risk they assume by operating in extremely dangerous environments also turns them into easy targets, especially if they are the subjects of negative reports in the media.

On the other hand, we need to acknowledge that our own attitudes and practices must be partly to blame. Paying attention to the rules and customs of businesses run by the majority under similar circumstances could make life much easier. It could also help us in protecting ourselves from falling prey to danger.

For example, hiring someone from one's own community who needs a job and otherwise could not find it elsewhere because he or she is perceived as 'different,' may certainly be good for both parties, provided one doesn't break the laws of the land. But cutting corners here and there to fatten one's own pockets is neither ethical nor legal. It might bring short-term gains, but such practices can neither bring peace nor satisfaction. However, it certainly will bring a bad name to the community.

Maintaining cleanliness of the kitchens and bathrooms in our Desi-owned restaurants can win many more laurels from the customers and may bring more business, the ultimate bottom line for a businessman, simply because restaurants usually thrive on word-of-mouth advertising.

As far as personal behavior is concerned, care for our fellow citizens, neighbors, and colleagues should always be paramount in our minds. The comfort zone of others must not be violated. Spoken communication must be soft and slow enough for native English-speakers to understand our accents. The rules of driving must be adhered to. The etiquette of polite dining must be respected. Tips to waiters and waitresses should reflect the norms of the restaurant. Saving money on tips is never a good practice. It leaves a bad impression in the minds of servers, especially if the 'served-ones' happen to belong to a minority community.

When using public transportation and elevators, priority needs to be given to those in need, such as the elderly and the disabled. We need to maintain discipline and control over young children just as the natives do. Letting children run wild in mixed social gatherings reflects badly on the community at-large. Shouting loudly in public places and talking incessantly in movie theaters as well as in religious and social functions are habits that need to be avoided. It is ill-mannered to speak in one's native tongue in the immediate presence of people who do not understand that language.

Wherever people gather, be it a neighborhood, a park, a place of employment or the mall, all eyes will naturally fall on members of minorities. The minorities stand out simply because they are different from what is generally considered 'local norms.' This is all the more reason for those of us who belong to such minority groups to maintain extra vigilance and be little more sensitive as to how our behavior is perceived by those in the majority.

Like it or not, as members of a minority group, we must "bend over backwards" and "walk the extra mile." We must do better than our neighbors and peers just to be accorded the same level of respect. This is our responsibility to us, not to mention the community at-large. Being a resident or a citizen of a country like the U.S. automatically grants one with many rights and many opportunities, of which the fruits can be plentiful. Yet to truly enjoy the taste, it is our individual responsibility to nurture the newly planted trees - our new lifes in the new environment of the adopted homeland - with utmost care and to the best of our abilities. Should we not act appropriately and quickly, it might well turn out to be too late for all of us and the tree might simply shrivel away?

28.
Converting the Golden Years into Real Gold

In the early 70s, many professional Indians migrated to United States. Given their educational backgrounds and qualifications, it was not unusual for most of them to become very successful in their chosen professions or businesses. They became financially very well off and thus were able to live their 'American Dreams' in the literal sense of this phrase. Their children have grown up and now are either in colleges or have already graduated. Others may already have married children while the children of many more will be tying knots, and thus their nests will be empty soon, if they are not already so. Therefore, the majorities of the immigrants are either nearing retirement or have already been rocking their chairs for a while in the patios or the porches of their houses.

Like many other Americans of the same age, albeit with some differences, the Indian expatriates are forced to wonder, "What next?" This question forces them to consider the checks and balances of their lives that they have lived here. Such perusals may also help in planning a strategy for realizing mental peace and satisfaction without any guilt as they march slowly towards their so-called 'Golden Years.' This strategy has nothing to do with financial planning nor is it a lead in for unsolicited medical advice. What people are looking for – and what they need -- is a strategy to turn their 'Golden Years,' into fruitful purpose otherwise these years have the potential of turning into cheap and dull brass, full of frustration.

During the working years, one is busy supporting one's family. The concerns about these 'Golden Years' usually take a back seat to more immediate issues. The majority of Indians do not develop hobbies as they require time and money, both of which are consumed by the needs of their growing families. First-generation Indian-Americans also do not carry any great desire for evening ball games. A few might show some interest in golf or tennis to stay fit, but these again are activities that many will not participate in.

Involvement in religious affairs, though important for some, may not be considered useful by others. Those who have been in the Western countries for a while develop a kind of aversion to such an involvement. Many are turned off by the constant, ego-driven battles for leadership on the turfs of religious places, where mud-slinging is the norm rather than the exception. Some individuals might get interested in politics, but they are few and far between, and given their minimal electoral bank, the efforts have still to show fruitful results.

For many expatriates, the U.S., Canada, U.K., or some other Western country will be the final stop, whether one may like it or not. Our sunset years need to be utilized to keep our minds busy with constructive work. Such involvement can help the communities of our adopted lands while setting a good example for our cousins back home. Needy people just don't exist in India only. To keep thinking about back home where not many of us will take our last breath is at best a wishful dream. If one looks around, there is a great need for taking care of the homeless, the sick and otherwise helpless people right here in our adopted homelands. These individuals have the same problems and needs as many folks back home do, only the environment and culture makes them appear different.

There are several homeless shelters in every town. Many elderly retired individuals donate their money and time towards taking care of the needy. Hospitals and nursing homes are full of indigenous elderly volunteers pushing wheelchairs and carts helping needy patients and residents with their feeding and cleaning. However, rarely does one see one of our own among them. A recent study about volunteer services in America reported that 44% of American adults did some sort of volunteer work in year 2000, putting in about 15.5 billion hours. These 84 million volunteers contributed about 24 hours each month. When one looks at these numbers, it becomes glaringly obvious that people of Eastern communities are not doing their parts at all.

Some of us try to send our children to volunteer their services at hospitals and nursing homes, but such motivation is often driven by a need to ensure our children's chances for a better career rather than instilling the concept of service as a civic duty. Besides, as important as it is for children to develop habits of civic service, isn't a habit of such service all the more important for retirees? The retirees of south Asian backgrounds have the time, the education, the experience and the financial resources to be equally more effective and helpful. Professional Indians do not have problems in communicating and don't have much of a language barrier.

By providing company to elderly individuals, one could brighten the long and lonely days of those compromised elderly souls, destined to spend their last days in the dark and unending convoluted corridors of long-term health care facilities.

Another way to bring comfort to the needy while seeking self satisfaction is in serving hot dinners to the homeless at various shelters. These kinds of services do not require large sums of money or skill. Instead, members of the Indian diaspora can help in fulfilling their civic responsibilities by serving at these facilities and prove to the community in which they live that they are as much committed to their new homeland as those whose families arrived 300 and 400 years ago. More to the point, the satisfaction one draws from such involvement is beyond belief. It cannot be described; one can only feel it. By helping the needy in this way, we can set a morally-desirable example for our progeny, for which it always will be thankful.

There are lots of other avenues through which involvement in public service can make a difference. Becoming members and leaders of groups – Non-Government Organizations or "NGOs" – such as those affiliated with or run by the World Health Organization and others that are involved with eradicating world hunger, as well as supporting orphanages, population control groups, hygiene groups, literacy centers and others- can go a long way in helping the citizens of the world.

One could also look into many other domestic organizations that always stand ready to accept volunteers. Going into neighborhood schools and helping teachers and students with their daily school work, benefits society and makes our presence felt as an involved and community-oriented group. Plenty of information about a community's needs in relation to one's profession is readily available through various governmental and community-sponsored volunteer agencies. All one needs to do is to show a desire and take the plunge.

The president of United States, in the recent past, has called for Americans to volunteer their times to various non-profit institutions, organizations, religious centers and community centers. This call applies as much to Indian-Americans as to Italian-Americans, German-Americans and Hispanic-Americans or for that matter every other hyphenated-American.

In large cities with a huge population of immigrants from India, there are many newly-arrived elderly immigrants, brought in as dependent parents by their children. They end up sitting idle at home all day while the bread earning children are at work. Isolated by age, language, and culture, these recently arrived elderly immigrants are desperate for social interaction. Giving them company and taking them to the social events of their interests can greatly brighten their days and ease the pain of these lonely and forgotten groups of individuals.

Stated simply, the 'Golden Years' turn gold, only if one's time is used appropriately. It is up to us. We can sit home and watch the world pass us by during our mature years on earth, or we can take advantage of our health, our financial resources and intellectual capabilities by using them in ways that can brighten the lives of those around us and within whom darkness abounds. These kinds of useful works will help us reap mental and spiritual satisfaction, while at the same time serve as shining examples for our future generations.

Serving one's own self and children alone is not the only purpose of human life, for such behavior is common among all living creatures. In fact, what sets us apart from the rest of God's creation is how we, as human beings, try our best to make this world better for all, regardless of where one happens to be on the totem pole. Caring for one's own self at this age, through myriad of exercises and leisurely pursuits is certainly essential but taking part in the well-being of others in need should not be ignored either. It is easy to light another candle with the one that is still lit. But a faltering light, left alone, will end up becoming part of the darkness that surrounds it. It is for us now to choose.

29.

On Culture and Faith

The culture of any given country draws its strengths and weaknesses as well as its customs and traditions from the written and unwritten codes of the faith of its majority people. This is true all over the world. Among the plethora of the faiths that trace their roots to India, Hinduism remains the most predominant religion. Therefore, most of the people of India, regardless of their ethnicities or places of residence, naturally happen to be surrounded by the believers of this faith. It is therefore, but natural that the cultures, traditions and customs of the minority groups in India, irrespective of their own faiths, are under the direct influence of the faith of its majority i.e. the Hinduism.

Most of the people of the Indian subcontinent do not truly confront the issue of distinguishing their faiths from their cultures in their daily routine. In fact in their minds, faith and culture seem to overlap. The line where religion ends and confront the issue of distinguishing their faiths from their cultures in their daily routine. In fact in their minds, faith and culture seem to overlap. The line where religion ends and culture begins is very fine, at times obscure and may even be totally extinct in the thought process of many Indians.

The Eastern immigrants who settled in the West, first came in direct contact with the predominantly Judeo-Christian traditions of their adopted homelands only after migration. The conflicts were not evident as long as the followers of the so-called "exotic religions of the East" as Westerners labeled them, stayed within the guidelines established for them by the culture of the majority. But when immigrants started to cross the fine line of practicing their faiths and cultures without staying sensitive to the feelings of the natives, the trouble started to brew. The latter got the impression that the immigrants were trying to impose their imported styles of living upon them. This brought intercultural conflicts into the open. Regardless of the permissiveness and open-mindedness of this society, it is difficult for the people to accept the imposition of different faiths or cultures upon their indigenous established values.

Modern technology has truly shrunk the present world. The mobility of people as well as the exchange of ideas and philosophy has become commonplace. The North American and European countries are gradually becoming inundated with people migrating from the East. They are bringing with them the baggage of their own cultures and faiths. Eastern religious institutions are sprouting all over western countries, resulting in a significant change in the religious landscape of the West. If one explores the historical perspectives, one comes to realize that the same kinds of transformations were encountered when Christianity and Western culture was imposed on the societies of the East.

Arguments are often made that the U.S. and Canada

are both the lands of immigrants, and that even the people belonging to the majority Christian faith are not native to this country. The Eastern immigrants with their non-Judeo-Christian backgrounds often state "If the Christians can do certain things, why can't we? And besides, did not the Europeans treat the Indian subcontinent and its culture in the same way when they first arrived in India and subjugated us? So what is the problem?" While there may be some truth here, at best it is only a limited truth.

We need to differentiate between our desire to live our culture and the manner in which we go about it. In doing so, we must not forget to fully honor the culture of the society we have adopted as our own and in which we have decided to live. In part, the answer resides in subtle adjustments as to how we practice our culture here without crossing the boundaries of our own faith. However, to do this we must determine where the boundary of a given culture stops and that of the faith begins and vice versa.

The practice of a faith back home naturally included intrusions of the culture in which it was being practiced but such intrusions were the consequence of a slow process over a period of many centuries. Therefore, more often than not they were imperceptible. New environments with different value systems in the adopted homelands of the West naturally lead to a feeling of persecution among the practitioners of transplanted faiths. At times it gives them the impression that the established guidelines of their faiths are being violated and their religious traditions are being trampled upon intentionally, when generally speaking, such might not be the case. It is important to remember this popular saying in this regard, "When in Rome, do as the Romans do." This statement in all probability refers to culture, but I do not recall anybody ever saying, 'Practice your faith in Rome, the way Romans do.'

Most native populations and the host cultures in multi-faith Western societies are usually not bothered by immigrants having their own places of worship. They let newer immigrants practice their religions the way they deem fit, as long it is done without interfering with the lifestyles of the indigenous population. It is only when the host cultures feel threatened by foreign cultures, the trouble ensues. When the immigrants start using their religious places for things other than religious services, it becomes a cause for concern and rightly so. Playing partisan politics inside religious places with loud arguments may lead to violence necessitating the intrusion of law enforcement agencies. Under any circumstance, such behaviors must not be allowed inside a sanctuary and should, therefore, be totally banned.

There are countless examples where cultural traditions inadvertently mix with religious practices, leading to confusion that could be easily avoided by having a bit of clarity between the two.

For example, cremation of a deceased individual is required by the Hindu and Sikh faiths. However, cremation using an open pyre, as one does in India, is a cultural tradition and perhaps not an absolute requirement of either of the faiths as far as I know. The laws of this country do not allow the use of open fire for cremation even if it were possible. In this case, one can accommodate Western laws by modifying the traditional practice (using an indoor crematorium rather than outdoor pyre), and one can easily do so without violating the requirements of one's faiths.

Similarly, a turban for a Sikh is part of his religious requirement; it must be worn by a conforming Sikh. A turban may be an odd sight to Westerners, but it is not an intrusion and has been normally accepted by most of the people, at least up until the horrible events of 9-11. Removing a turban is worrisome, if it has to be removed just to please non-Sikhs, including the people of India. It should be noted here that many Indian people belonging to other faiths may also not attach the same significance to a turban that a Sikh does.

The loose dress worn by men and women in India is a cultural tradition that can easily be modified provided it is not ordained by a particular faith. We all know that political leaders of India, the present and past, including the late Prime Minister Jawahar Lal Nehru, dressed in the customary Indian dresses while in India but changed to three-piece suits complete with designer ties on their visits to the West. Vegetarianism is a requirement of certain Eastern faiths; it is not optional. On the other hand, eating with one's hands is a cultural and not a religious tradition and as such it is best avoided in the company of Westerners.

One of the reasons for the present crisis in the world is the fundamental philosophical differences between the faiths of the East and that of the West. Eastern religions, most of the time, emphasize that one must endeavor throughout one's entire life to attain Mukti or salvation for the soul from the cycle of life and death and be merged with One. The people of the East are coached day in and day out that this is the only purpose of human life and whatever is done in life, should be done with this aim in mind. To that end, different religions of the East suggest that one must not indulge excessively in worldly affairs. Some of the faiths even ask their followers for the renunciation of worldly comforts, even to the point of torturing the human body.

The people of the West, on the other hand, rather put great emphasis on worldly comforts in the present life, the life they are living today. They emphasize issues like youth, beauty and the biologic needs, much of which is taboo in Eastern faiths. An old person in the West is often considered dispensable, a useless and wasteful commodity that is a burdensome liability on the family and on society. "The young people have to live their own lives instead of worrying about the problems of the older members of the family," is a statement often heard in many contexts from all quarters of the West. On the contrary, the Eastern culture emphasizes respect for elders. The life experiences of the elderely are to be given due importance. They need to be listened to, understood, respected and accommodated.

Understanding and addressing these differences in their own contexts should ease the minds of people from both cultures. Minor adjustments and compromises in the way one practices one's culture in adopted homelands can go a long way in smoothing out the wrinkles and aligning it with the prevalent values and traditions of the West. This will ultimately lead to less tension and less of the shoulder rubbing between the two cultures. However such compromises or adjustments need not ignore the fundamental established practices and requirements of one's faith.

This attitude will help the immigrants from the East integrate better into the multi-faith environments in which they have chosen to live in the West, thus making life easier for both Easterners and Westerners.

30.

India, Indians and Environmental Cleanliness

Walking through the corridors of my hospital one day, I encountered a situation that many of us come across every day, a situation that usually sails past our eyes, unnoticed and unregistered.

An invalid in a wheelchair, barely able to move his body, was trying with great difficulty to push himself along the corridor in front of me. This person noticed a small piece of paper lying on the impeccably clean tiles of the hospital floor. He stopped, took a deep breath, and with great effort tried to pick up that little piece of paper. Noticing the difficulty he was having, and assuming that the paper he was trying to retrieve was something he had dropped, I bent to assist him. To my surprise he said "Thank you, doc! Thanks for your help," and then continued, "It gives me a tremendous amount of pain when people show their apathy towards keeping public places clean and neat. After all, we human beings have a responsibility to keep our environments in shape. Isn't it what makes a man different from other animals?"

My mind flashed back to an incident that occurred several years ago during one of our family's visits back home. While traveling from New Delhi to Punjab, we observed another car traveling ahead of us. Strangely enough, the riders of that car had flown to India on the same flight we had taken. About fifty miles into the countryside, while our car was overtaking this vehicle, a banana peel flew from the open window of the car ahead of us and went through the open window of our car, landing on my son's lap. Obviously, we were annoyed and stopped our car, as did the other car. The mother of the boy who threw the banana peel out the window instantaneously apologized on behalf of her son. She stated that her son was trying to throw the skin onto the roadside when the wind blew it into our car. Needless to say, her explanation was accurate, so I was ready to drop the matter. However, my son who was barely 12 years old, continued, "But why should your son try to throw the banana peel on the roadside to begin with? Would you let him do this kind of thing abroad, in the country you just came from?"

It was a strong comment that took the lady by surprise. I tried to quiet down my son. However he kept on and said, "Dad, it's not a question of as to why it fell on me and not on the intended target. The issue is why was it thrown out of the window in the first place? Are there not already heaps and heaps of open garbage on either side of the road?" I saw his point, and it occurred to me that if each and every citizen of India would concern himself or herself with such matters, India would be one of the most beautiful countries of the world to live in. We have the people and we have the cleaning equipments and still we have all this mess. I could not help but wonder why the NRIs behave the way they do when it comes to the cleanliness of the environment, especially back home in India?

Is the attitude and lack of concern displayed towards environmental cleanliness by the woman and her son a part of our cultural heritage? Is that what makes us leave the cleaning jobs to the poorest segments of our society? Or do we let things stay dirty because we believe that in India, anything goes? Could it be that we lack the understanding about the not-so-obvious health consequences of our actions? Or is it due to all of the above factors?

We are all aware of the pathetic scenes that are often portrayed in the streets of India. One notices heaps of garbage getting larger every day, while open sewer lines stay clogged in the streets in front of houses and businesses. The residents are not bothered by throwing the refuse into the streets outside of their homes, believing that if the inside of the house is clean, that is all what matters. In fact, at many places, it indeed is part of the lifestyle in India. Little do we realize that the flies and mosquitoes know very well how to fly inside the home from the heaps of garbage lying open outside of the houses? They bring with them the germs of Cholera, Typhoid, Dengue fever and other killer diseases of summer. The diseases and illnesses inflicted by these little creatures do not discriminate between the rich and the poor; all are equal in their eyes.

One may argue that the upkeep of the streets, alleys and open areas is the responsibility of local civic authorities and that residents should not have to bother themselves with such mundane concerns. But as with all other governmental affairs, street cleaners and other sanitation workers often end up working half-heartedly, just to keep the system afloat. Several times in a year, this most important civic function stands still in many towns and cities. Strikes and 'bandhs' are frequently announced by the employees and politicians trying to highlight and bring their selfish interests home to the rest of the public. The poorest citizens are left to their own fates, suffering all the time while keeping alive their hope for a miraculous reprieve from their misery. The cleaning crews are usually found picking up the garbage from the doorsteps of the politician's houses, as they have been ordered to do so, while it keeps on rotting in front of the residences of the ordinary citizens.

India's caste system also has a role to play in our negative attitude towards the environment. The centuries-old distaste for manual labor prevents us from our responsibilities in keeping our environments clean through our physical efforts. Well-established people usually do not concern themselves with the physical labor required in maintaining a clean and healthy environment, for that is considered below their dignity. From early childhood, the Indian culture indirectly reinforces the belief that manual labor is only appropriate for the humblest of the castes. An attitude of not taking an active part in environmental cleanliness and leaving it for the less-fortunate ones is usually seen as status symbol. We are raised to believe that well-established people -- the so-called 'rich gentry' -- need not bother with these undignified chores; instead it is to be taken care of by the household servants.

Such strange anomalies of Indian culture become readily apparent but only after we have been exposed to the dignity that Western culture assigns to manual labor. Of course, I must quickly add here that this is not necessarily true with all the Indians all the time for TV and news-media have made the world shrink tremendously.

The personal freedom in India about which we constantly boast about and give sermons to others, has altogether a different connotation for many people in India. To them, it may imply that being an Indian in India means that one is free to let the historical monuments, the streets, the roadsides, and their attendant environments remain dirty. To others, it suggests that it is okay to illegally occupy a plot of land under the excuse of erecting a religious place, or to create slums by building unauthorized structures without civic approval and then paying no heed, whatsoever, to the environmental cleanliness.

The politicians and highly-placed government officials also have the full freedom to expand their personal territorial fortunes by illegally grabbing the land and putting up illegal structures that may not be in congruence with environmental concerns. This may even come at the expense of poor neighbors who, unfortunately have no say in this matter. Yet it is not okay for the authorities to stop their proliferation or to dismantle them, for the politicians and their vote banks are the ultimate authority.

After all, we happen to be a free people of a free country. Yet through all of this, we seem to forget that until and unless we use our freedom for the purpose of uplifting the lives of the ordinary citizens of India and maintain its beauty and environmental cleanliness, the freedom of India could remain hollow. Having said so, there is a need to acknowledge the recent appearance of a silver lining on the horizon as evidenced by rapid development in several sectors.

Our religions usually provide good guidance for making our lives happier in the next life. But we somehow manage to interpret and rationalize, and that too without any true religious dictum, that it is okay to ignore the ugly and unhealthy environments of our present life. We seem to forget the fact that the purpose of a religion is not only limited to prepare us for the next life. Rather, an equally important function of our faiths happens to be taking care of the most pressing needs of our present life. Keeping our environments neat and tidy so as to avoid disease and sickness certainly could not be considered against any such goal.

Only a neat and healthy environment can ensure a healthy body in which a mind full of true spirituality can then flourish. That is why the Eastern faiths have always dictated the significance of cleanliness in the attainment of ultimate "Higher Truth." Shouldn't it then naturally follow that clean environments be once again considered as our prime responsibility as ordained by our faiths, faiths that we otherwise so passionately believe in, feel proud of and often talk loudly about, especially when we happen to be away from our countries of birth?

31.
I Love my India!

"I love my India" were the words my sister-in-law would often pronounce whenever we asked her to spend more time with us during her visits to America. Her son and his family are citizens of U.S. and have been living here for a while. Yet, she always wanted to go back soon after she will arrive here for a visit because she missed India, her home, desperately. The fact is that such sentiments are deeply ingrained not only in the minds of short-term visitors of the Indian subcontinent to the West but among almost every NRI who has made his or her home abroad permanently. The longing to visit parents, relatives and friends becomes extreme, as time passes by. One keeps hope alive to return back whenever an opportunity arises for there always remains a sense of incompleteness without such visits.

On arrival in India and meeting with the family members

waiting on the curbsides of the airports always creates a moment that uniquely combines a sense of pleasure with excitement that can only be felt but not described. After one starts heading home, either by a personal vehicle of the family members of the NRI, a hired taxi, or a bus, the reality of death trap set up by the killer Indian traffic starts showing its ugly head.

India is on the road to progress but not necessarily the travel on its roads. India rightly claims itself to be on the pinnacle of world in information technology but it sinks to the bottom in terms of road safety for those who helped it reach there. Indian political leaders are busy in telling the world at the top of their voices that India is shining, but the shine turns pale with the innocent blood lost on its highways and byways. India has scientists who are no less in numbers and in their achievements than any other country of the world, but the numbers of avoidable deaths on the road side also do not seem to lag behind. We have one of the biggest democracies of the world but the practice of democracy in driving without paying attention to the rules of travel on roads leads to large numbers of death and dying.

Due to advancement in medical field, we have become one of the few countries in the world where the health management groups from other nations wish to outsource their patients for treatment. Still many travelers die on road side precisely due to lack of first aid in medical care. We are the call-center of the world. Our currency is getting stronger and stronger and our mobile phone technology has awakened up to the needs of country at a much rapid pace than many advanced countries. A good number of the richest men of the world happen to be Indians but poverty in rules of driving is in stark evidence. There has been enough ammunition to be proud of our motherland and we should. Yet, it seems that something is amiss in the progress of India that lets its sons and daughters bleed to death unnecessarily on the road side.

In order to understand this issue in its proper perspective, one simply needs to look at the losses suffered by one's own family members in day to day travel on the killer roads of India. Ask any person, NRI or otherwise, and it becomes obvious that one or more of the relatives or friends have unnecessarily perished on those deadly roads from the accidents. He or she will also tell you that the injured souls could have been saved had some passer-by picked up the courage and helped the victim in getting timely medical help. The apathy and lack of concern shown by the onlookers adds to the misery and may lead to the demise of those who otherwise might still have been roaming on this earth. Such a behavior though not justifiable, is easily explainable and I will allude to it later in this essay.

My personal family has suffered the fates of many other unfortunate helpless Indians. My sister-in-law, the lady who could not wait to go back home for she loved every moment of her life in India, became a mere statistics in one of those fatal road accidents. Her daughter-in-law also died along with her in the same accident, just because the driver of the other vehicle who hit their car decided to travel in the wrong direction of a divided highway. In fact, during the last several years, I have lost five members of my very close family to this killer disease, including my brother, my nephew, my brother-in-law as well as very two recent members mentioned above. And as stated above I am not the only one affected, almost every Indian has been. Yet it doesn't have to be that way.

Statistically speaking, the situations and prevailing driving conditions on the roads of India are very grim, to say the least. For example, India has roughly about 1% of the world's vehicular population, yet it leads the world with an incidence of 6-10% of the global road accidents. Every year, there are over 300,000 road accidents in which almost close to 100,000 people die. Meera Gupta, a teacher at St. Peter's college, quotes in one of the Internet sites that 'More people die on the road accidents in India than by disease, cancer or HIV.' National Transportation Planning and Research Center (NTPRC) reports, "The number of road accidents in India is three times higher than those that may occur in the developed countries." Keep in mind though, that not all accidents are reported or included in statistics in India, The real numbers of tragedies will have to be higher, given our style of reporting.

No doubt then, the Bureau of Consular Affairs, U.S. Department of State in its Consular information sheet relating to the Traffic safety and Road conditions rightly warns the potential visitors to India that "The travel by road in India is dangerous." It hesitates not in advising that "the safest driving policy is to always assume that the other drivers will not respond to a traffic situation in the same way one would in the United States." If further states that on the Indian roads "Might makes it Right" What it implies essentially through this statement is that bigger the vehicle, such as a bus or over-loaded truck, lesser the responsibility it will assume and greater the freedom it will have in breaking the rules of traffic, like running the red lights or ignoring the traffic signs, provided there are any. Decimating a living Indian into dust is 'a business-routine in India.'

Merging directly into the traffic from cross roads is the norm and there are no signs to stop it, most of the time. Even if there is one which might have survived the wrath of vandalism or theft, no one really cares to read it or follow what it says. Even if the highway is divided, the driver will seem not to care or hesitate in traveling against the direction and that too without lights. In fact, two recent family deaths in head-on collision of their car were indeed the result of a tractor-trolley being driven by its young amateur driver in the wrong direction.

The Indian roads were not designed for the present modes of transportation. Overloaded trucks and buses, trolleys with overhanging canopies bringing crops from the villages to the markets in the cities, cars and taxies, scooters, motor cycles and auto rickshaws all compete on the same road but with their own speed. At the same time man-driven cycle-rickshaws, bicycles, carts pulled by oxen, camels and many others, all share the same road. Elephant-riders en route to weddings as well as independent strolling live-stocks, including our sacred cows, stray dogs, pigs, hordes of sheep and pedestrians do not wish to stay behind either. One might question as to why government will not intervene and do something about this? Answers are there but only for those who wish to care.

First of all, the government is not run by aliens from the outer space. They are the same people belonging to the same stock as the rest of the population. The attitudes and behaviors of the decision makers, like the people they are supposed to serve, become self centered as soon as they take the command. Should an honest soul decide to intervene, there won't be any funds available simply because people do not wish to pay taxes. It is well-known that the money collected will only warm the pockets of the men-in-power rather than government treasury. At the same time, the nature of the needed mega projects truly defies human imagination. And as to following the rules, it is next to impossible for the freedom in India implies in breaking the rules of law for everything, including traffic rules.

Leaving injured on the roadsides of India to die unattended and without emergency medical aid is a common occurrence.

Passing by traffic and the pedestrians try not to act "Good Samaritans." The fear of police harassment for those who may claim to have witnessed the scene of accident or offered help to the dying victims keeps them away from intervening. Repeated trips to police stations and courts essentially turn a witness into a culprit itself.

The driver of a vehicle, who may accidently cause injury to a pedestrian, to a sacred cow or cause damage to a vehicle usually tries to run away from the site of the accident. He or she is scared of being roughened up, seriously maimed, or even killed by the passers-by or by the family of the victim. The other innocent occupants of the accident-causing vehicle, for no fault of theirs, could meet the same fate by the angry mob that often tries to take law in its own hands.

Many lives can be saved by creating an environment where the harassment of the witness could be prevented. Collecting legal evidence at the site of an incident and fully rewarding the witness for the time wasted, rather than bothering him or her for rest of the life, will truly serve the justice and help the law. It will also save many lives that simply go down the drain for lack of timely medical help. Behavioral modification by offering rewards to witnesses should be encouraged through television and print news-media. This might change the trend and make people more willing to offer help without any fear of personal harassment.

If human life is to be considered worth a penny, then a serious thought towards safety on the road must be demanded as a basic human right by each and every citizen of India. Creating tough rules for issuing driving licenses, especially to the underage and ineligibles drivers and making driving test mandatory, indeed will be the first step. But it shouldn't stop here. Punishing the law breakers not only on paper but in real time and to the extent of the law, should be made something like a religious requirement. Tougher problems demand tougher solutions.

Certainly more roads in tune with the present modes of transportation are needed. Asking for them, however, or even dreaming about is a tall order here and it would be like asking for a miracle to happen. Simple behavioral changes for safe driving and framing laws that encourage passers-by to get involved at the site of accident without fear of repercussion certainly doesn't appear to be asking too much. A single life saved will be blessings all too many.

32.

About Indian Parties and Gifts

Immigrants from the world over, regardless of the duration of their stay in the adopted lands, always carry an urge to meet with other people from their homelands, especially on weekends and evenings. To this end, they have developed a system where all occasions, significant or not, are used for celebrations in private homes or in rental halls. This is not to say that members of the diaspora didn't have parties or gatherings in their homelands. However, relatively speaking, these kinds of celebratory parties are more common here especially within the immigrant communities than they were and probably are still back home.

One reason for the frequency of these gatherings in the

West is the inherent disconnect between the cultures of the immigrants' adopted countries as opposed to the cultures that they brought with them from the countries of their birth. Whether we like to say it or not, each one of the immigrants suffers from varying degrees of cultural deprivation. These parties offer an environment of nostalgia within which we can mingle, talk about our past and discuss back home politics.

Most of us arrange these parties for special occasions such as the birthday of a child, the marriage of a son or daughter, a house warming, or the purchase of a new business, and so forth. Regardless, each of us must present a gift to the host as demanded by culture, etiquette and common courtesy.

When we sit back and look around, we notice that sometimes, we buy or take gifts to the host family that might not have any use for us personally and which, given the situation, we would not like to have for ourselves. No doubt most or all of us repeatedly receive gifts that mean little to us. Fine china, crystal bowls and other gifts are opened up and then immediately returned to the containers they arrived in, where they often stay in storage until the first opportunity arises for us to recycle them onwards. I am not exactly sure about the percentage of individuals who could really use these sorts of gifts, but almost all of us who have lived here for a while seem to have collected an abundance of such items, items that are simply collecting dust in our garages or basements.

This happens mostly because we rarely put much thought into what the host really needs or what is truly going to be useful to him or her before we select our gift. Also, who wants to take time out of one's busy schedule to sit down for a thoughtful consideration and then go out from shop to shop and buy a gift for somebody else, be it a friend or a relative? Whatever is available in one's house gets quickly wrapped in a fresh shining wrapper, ready to be delivered as a gift. When the host opens the gift, his or her lips might say "Oh! Beeauuuuu….tiful! What a nice gift," especially in the presence of the guest who brought the gift. But in his or her mind it might well be another story.

This is hardly unique to immigrant Indians in the West. I observed this same kind of phenomenon about twenty-five years ago in India. One of my acquaintances showed me a closet full of lower-quality ladies dresses and saaris that were kept separate from rest of her garments. On my repeated questioning about what the clothing was for, she finally blurted out, *"Lainai, theinai kaa Samaan Hai,"* or, "these articles are for use as gifts only."

Taking bottles of wine as a gift for a host, especially, during house-warming parties, is also very popular among the people of our adopted homeland. It does not seem to have any Indian roots and is primarily a uniquely Western cultural practice. But listen to this; we the people of India have also started taking wine bottles to the houses of friends or relatives who might not even drink alcoholic beverages and therefore, may not have any use for them. In fact, wine is rarely consumed at Indian parties. Rather, the emphasis most of the time seems to be on scotch and other whiskeys and that too, preferably Chivas Regal or Johny Walker. Therefore, even from that perspective, wine has limited value as a gift.

A true gift to the host will be the one that the host could put to a good use and feel happy about receiving it. Providing tools of information about one's culture, one's religious faith, and one's native country in the form of books, videotapes, or DVDs can serve the dual purpose of giving a gift, while also disseminating basic knowledge about our roots. This in turn will help make our lives and our children's lives a bit easier in our adopted land. A candle can light another candle, and that candle can further light many more candles without losing its own glow. Not only the recipient, but the entire family, can learn more about things they did not know before. There are many good books about India, its culture and various Indian religions that could be used for the purpose of gift giving.

Likewise, when it comes to giving gifts to Indian friends, one could consider a book about the history or culture of our adopted homelands, as many of us tend to be very ignorant in this field. If interests of the intended recipient are known before-hand, one can choose the book accordingly. Gifting a book, a video or a DVD doesn't cost any more than a normal gift and the cost is almost always within the budget of everybody, irrespective of the occasion.

I am sure there are many other creative methods by which one could make gift-giving and gift-receiving an occasion of immense pleasure and usefulness. Gift-giving should not be perceived as a burdensome chore that one has to perform. One just needs to sit down with a thoughtful mind and assess the needs of the host prior to purchasing a gift. A well-thought out gift not only brings immense pleasure to the recipient, but can indirectly provide valuable information and knowledge. It also makes the recipient cherish such a gift for many years to come and share it with others once he or she has used it rather than storing an unneeded item in the garage or basement. Nothing could be more satisfying than this thoughtful action on the part of a gift-giver.

33.

'Snakes in the Hole' or Snacks in the Hall

.

A few years ago, one of my American acquaintances, while praising the entrepreneurial spirit of the people of the Indian subcontinent, mentioned a joke in relation to their Indian accent. His intent was not malicious at all. Indeed, he was trying to compliment the people of the Indian subcontinent, who, in spite of their occasional heavy accent and other race-related issues, have been very successful the world over in their chosen professions. He went on to relate his experience about a party where the Indian host had asked him to pick up 'snacks from the hall' before sitting down at his assigned table. This American acquaintance confided in me that it sounded to him as if the Indian host was referring to some 'snakes in the hole.' Obviously he had difficulty in figuring it out, but upon fully comprehending the statement of the Indian host, he ended up having a hearty laugh.

Interestingly, this Indian host, a well known person in the community, happened to be a very successful businessman in spite of his thick and oftentimes difficult to understand accent. The American acquaintance apologetically mentioned that accents of Indian people at-large is very understandable. Yet his joke proved a point that in the matter of accents or verbal expressions even well-settled immigrants from the Indian subcontinent may have a long way to go.

We live in a multicultural, multi-ethnic and multi-linguistic society. And yet the language that binds all of us together happens to be English. An understanding of English and the ability to communicate in it, therefore, assumes a great significance for all of us. Once a transplanted person starts living in U.S.A., Canada, U.K. and Australia or for that matter in any other English-speaking country, the skill in understanding and communicating in this language naturally improves. However, as far as an accent is concerned, it may improve to some extent yet it never goes away.

In the sixties, the Indians and other Asians who immigrated to this country belonged primarily to well-established professions, such as medicine and engineering or they were in the teaching profession. In addition, there were significant numbers of students in many universities and colleges. They had a varied level of competence in English and their accents largely depended not only upon the geographic area in which their childhood was spent but also upon the quality of schooling and medium of instruction in their formative years. Yet in those times, the Indians, like many other skilled and professional immigrants from elsewhere, were accepted easily and respected greatly for the culture of their hard work. This was irrespective of their communication skills or proficiency in the delivery of English.

As time passed the Indians, like other immigrant communities, started exploring other professions and business opportunities. Many became successful entrepreneurs in their own businesses and some opened their own companies while a few became CEOs of multinationals. Their skills kept on elevating them, finally bringing them to the forefront. With globalization of the world, and their built-in knowledge of the English language as well as their expertise in the upcoming information technologies, the Indian professionals became a force to reckon with.

However, as the pie kept on shrinking, the sailing didn't stay that smooth. With the addition of many non-skilled and non-professional people of Asian backgrounds, having a rather limited knowldege of English, arriving as piggy-backs on their previously settled relatives, the charisma of the times past was lost. As a consequence, the Asian immigrants seemed not to draw the same kind of respect that was afforded to their pioneer cousins.

In the multi-ethnic and multi-cultural society of the West, the ultimate success and acceptability of an immigrant is dependent, in part, on the proficiency of spoken English and accent. These factors are emphasized more in the corporate setting where interaction with the public is greater. A smart, skillful and highly educated individual, who otherwise could have reached the pinnacle of success without much difficulty, may now not get that far on the ladder of success if his or her accent is heavy. When being considered for a promotion, an immigrant's accent may turn out to be a silent determining factor in the ultimate fate. In teaching profession, in the universities and colleges, many-a-times, the talented professors could be passed over for tenure simply due to their accents. The speaking engagements would naturally not come their way with heavy accents as opposed to otherwise. Even in the business world, given every other consideration, the accent happens to be the main reason in the ultimate success of an immigrant.

The managers and supervisors at various enterprises are usually well aware and are fairly sensitive about the rules and regulations of hiring practices and discrimination based on color, creed and origin of birth. They are cognizant of the fact that the laws of the land could easily take them to task if such a practice were to be documented under their supervision. However, when it comes to communication, an individual with an accent might not find much respite, for it is not difficult to hide the obvious. It is not impossible for the employers to prove that the accent of a given employee is causing a hindrance in their ultimate bottom line, especially if it involves dealing with the public. This deficiency can be used as their last weapon in hiring or firing as well as chopping someone off from the job easily, which otherwise they might find it difficult to do so.

The inclusion of the English language at an early age in schools all over India is one reason that Indians are successful in the communication industry, surpassing many other rapidly developing nations. This has brought in a visible upswing in the establishment of many so-called 'call centers' in India. With an overflowing pool of English-speaking young men and women in India, the corporate employers of the West find many opportunities to tap into this easily available English-speaking pool. For their part, reasonably well-educated but unemployed Indian youths turn thankful for the opportunities that landed at their doorsteps almost inadvertently.

The world we live in is shrinking rapidly. In as far as methods of communications are concerned, the boundaries between different countries are fading, thanks to the onslaught of Internet. One could simultaneously watch and talk to the person sitting thousands and thousands of miles away. The geographic distances seem not to have much clout, as they used to at one time, due to the convenience of world-wide travel.

With the passage of time, it is becoming fairly obvious that the people with good communication skills in English and without a thick accent will end up having great days ahead in this global technology, notwithstanding other issues.

It is, therefore, essential that each and every member of the diaspora must pay heed to this aspect and do whatever needs to be done to help improve this deficiency to the extent possible. Any immigrant coming from any country at any age can improve chances of placement by improving his or her accent. It is easily doable without much cost. The help, if seriously sought, is always available. Those who understand and respect this golden rule of mastering the accent, will rule the rest, and the rest who don't, will have to rest at the bottom without much of a rest in the rest of their lives.

34.

Religious Congregations In the Homes of Indian Diaspora Members

The members of the Indian diaspora in Western countries often celebrate occasions of happiness by arranging religious functions at their homes. Such celebrations include a new house warmings, birthdays or marriages of their children, buying or selling of a business and many others. This is often done to seek blessings from God Almighty for that particular auspicious occasion or for offering gratitude for a successful fulfillment of an intended purpose. Likewise at the death of a close relative or during a personal loss of any kind, prayers are also arranged at the homes.

Looking back it seems that the celebrations at homes might have been relatively less prevalent in India than among the Indian diaspora living abroad. One could think of several reasons for such discrepancy. One likely explanation for this change in attitude is the easy availability of religious places of different faiths at every corner in India. Their abundance often makes it unnecessary to go through such an exercise at home. Additionally a lack of space in and around the house, coupled with narrow streets plus several other factors of Eastern lifestyles, all play their roles in making home celebrations somewhat difficult in India.

All along, we carried an impression about ourselves that we, the people of India, are the most religious people on earth. The validity of this perception suddenly dissipates on settling here and noting an abundance of churches and synagogues on every street corner. It further surprises us to realize that the religious places in the West are not entirely meant for religious services, the way we understood it back home. Rather, they are utilized for many other social activities and necessities.

The busy lifestyle of the West doesn't allow most of the people to perform religious services more than once a week, irrespective of their faiths. Being good imitators, the people of India try not to stay behind. However, a reduced frequency in religious engagements certainly limits the interaction with the religious friends, giving a perception that one is missing something. This obviously creates a need to arrange for such religious functions at home. Additionally, due to hard work and accompanying affluence, a higher proportion of the diaspora members are in a position to buy new homes at a relatively faster pace than it could have ever been possible in India. This further necessitates the desire for celebrations of religious functions for house warming. All these permutations and combinations create opportunities to have frequent religious services at the homes of the diaspora members.

Nothing is wrong with this good act. But the issue that I would like to draw attention to, in fact, relates to extending invitations to our Western neighbors or friends on such occasions. A good number of our people maintain friendly social contacts with their neighbors. However, an equal number of the members of diaspora seem to be fairly shy and tend not to mix well with the locals. Their relationship with neighbors may be limited to the extent of saying "hello" in passing and that too, while driving to or coming back from work.

Our Western neighbors are certainly aware of our weekend and evening social parties at home for they too arrange similar kinds of activities. In contrast, however, most of our Indian religious functions are usually held in the morning or daytime on the weekends. Consequently, our neighbors usually don't have much of an idea about their Indian neighbors' religious practices. Moreover, such practices are performed in ethnic languages and mediums that are totally foreign to them.

To add to their difficulties, we expect certain prerequisites from our neighbors that are totally alien to their daily lifestyles. For example, in the case of a Sikh function, it is expected by the host family that all the attendees take their shoes off, cover their heads and sit on the floor as a sign of respect to the "Guru Eternal," Guru Granth Sahib Ji. Yet the hosts usually do not take time prior to the arrival of their Western friends, who may not have one iota of knowledge in this regard, to explain to them what is expected.

The Westerners by nature are punctual and thus tend to arrive at the very beginning of the function, as should be the case. We, on the other hand, keep on gradually trickling in until the end of function. Entering the function when it is already in full swing doesn't make much sense to those who are not used to this kind of behavior. In their way of thinking, the purpose of an invitation for a religious function is to have a spiritual experience all the way through. For this to happen, the Western guests, not familiar with the Eastern

223

faiths, will naturally expect quietness without interruptions. When the atmosphere is not conducive, they end up enduring what they obviously perceive to be somewhat of an imposed punishment. The dilemma of these poor souls who feel stuck between a rock and a hard place is fairly obvious. Yet, the hosts often seem to exude a sense of achievement at having their neighbors over.

Does this mean that those who invite them should stop doing so? I do not believe this for a moment. Also does it mean that those who don't extend such invitations to their Western neighbors are wrong? Maybe or maybe not! However, it is only reasonable for the host families to show extra sensitivity to the plight and dilemma of such invited guests. After all, the basic purpose of an invitation, in part, happens to seek the company of the invited guests so that they can join with the host in a collective prayer. If what goes on is not understood by any of the invited guests, be they Indian or Westerner, the function is of no use to either of the parties.

I do not intend to suggest here that one has to change the style of the basic function or the language. Our religious scriptures happen to be in our mother language and translation into other languages, no matter how accurate, cannot do full justice. In case of the Sikh people, the *Gurbani*, as enshrined in Sri Guru Granth Sahib Ji, has come directly from our Gurus and other religious saints/Faquirs in the language that they spoke and no one is entitled to change or modify even a word of it. Yet there are ways to make things easier for those who do not comprehend what is being stated or performed at such functions.

In attending a Sikh function, sometimes back, at one of our family friend's home where a few of their Western neighbors were also present, I was impressed with the host family for the utmost sensitivity they displayed to their non-

Sikh guests. They asked this writer to spend a few minutes to explain in English what was happening, what it meant to the family for their guests to attend this function and what was expected of them? I must state that their invited guests were really pleased to learn about the function and thus did not feel excluded. In fact, their happiness and satisfaction led me to write about this topic.

Invited Western guests and neighbors should be informed in advance about the seating arrangement on the floor and the need to cover their heads if this happens to be a Sikh function. Other needed adjustments, as the faith of the host may demand, should be communicated upfront at the time of the invitation. A few soft cushions placed by the walls to provide support to the backs of the elderly guests suffering from arthrits, can definitely add to their comfort and earn goodwill for the host. If one cannot sit comfortably on the floor, there will be no interest in listening. The problem can also be circumvented, in part, by asking them to arrive as close to the end of ceremony as possible. This way, they will not get too tired and will not be distracted by watching the spectacle of late-arriving guests, walking into the function all the way to the end, as is usual in our functions.

The people of the East believe very strongly that their children should also attend these functions in order to become oriented to the faith. But by nature, children usually have their own agenda. They end up doing what they always do best, which is usually running around during the program and playing with their toys rather than sitting quietly or taking part in the function. The religious proceedings are usually beyond the comprehension of children, leading naturally to their boredom. It also causes a nuisance for the adults for it prevents them from paying heed to the ceremony.

Unfortunately, most of the host families do not make any arrangements for the children to stay busy during such functions. If one room could be allotted to the little children where they are kept under the watch of an adult it might solve the problem to an extent. As to the older children, they should be encouraged to sit with their parents to avoid disturbing others. After all, if our intent is to teach our children about our faith and its traditions, then we must make sure that they sit, see, listen, learn and allow others do the same. Ignoring children's religious needs at such times is an opportunity lost in orienting them to the basic tenets of our faith.

The practice of one's religion is a private and personal affair to begin with and celebrations, therefore, ought to be personal. Those who choose not to involve Western neighbors in their home religious functions should not feel any guilt. Those who do, should take a little time prior to the event to develop a plan for explaining the significance of the religious celebration. With a little preparation beforehand, the religious celebration will become memorable for the right reasons. This kind of gesture can certainly go a long way in building the long-term cordial relationship with neighbors. Without a proper attention to the sensitivities of the invited Western-guests, no good is done to anyone. Likewise, lending a serious ear to children' requirements can also help them learn more about their faith.

Needless to say that what is being discussed here is not new and many of us might well be practicing it already. Kudos to them!

35.

To Protest is Our Birthright, To Cause Mayhem is Not!

Who has ever said that life is a bed of roses? To live life is to accept all what comes along, the good and the bad, the happiness and the sadness, the pleasures and the pains, for after all it is a package deal. Sometimes we may get what we wish for, but oftentimes we don't. The material necessities of human lives are usually under the control of someone else, over and above the needy. A child's needs are usually met by parents. The adults have to work for their needs or else depend upon someone other than themselves. If one's demands are reasonable, those who are in positions of control will go along most of the time. But if our social, political or financial needs or demands seem beyond what those in control are willing or able to provide, frustrations usually ensue.

Conflicts arise when aggrieved parties are not able to get what they perceive to be rightfully theirs. Such conflicts are often the root cause for protests against the authorities or the people in control. Many people with Western orientations consider protests as their birthright and not an all out battle for life. On the other hand, the perception about protests among people of ethnic backgrounds, especially Asians, happens to be somewhat different. The Asians and most others who grew up outside of Western Europe and North America usually do not carry positive perception about authorities. We are all aware that protests of any kind in our homelands often turn into violent clashes. Such violent protests rarely lead to positive changes, no more than the Western styles of relatively benign protests.

From a conceptual point of view, the authorities, whosoever they might be, are 'supposed to' work for the people over whom they rule. In the past, most of the world was ruled by kings, queens and emperors who exerted complete authority and control over their subjects. In order to rule without trouble, such rulers made sure that the basic needs of their subjects were met. They knew that the stability of their thrones was directly proportional to the satisfaction of the people they ruled. If the people were too unhappy, it didn't take long for the thrones to tumble down. Over time, this equation has changed and such scenarios do not exist anymore. Not many kings, queens or emperors with absolute authorities over their subjects are left in this world. Those still in power, can easily be counted on the fingertips of one hand.

As times changed, so did the style of governance. Presently, the Western-style democracy has become the principal method of governance over a major part of the world. The democratic governments bring forth their own sets of regulations to which all concerned must adhere. No single individual has the degree of absolute authority or responsibility equivalent to that of bygone kings and queens. The elites of the ruling class are fully aware that their control upon the people is not dynastic or absolute. Rather, their authority is shared among several layers and as such the responsibilities have also become limited. In order to run governments successfully, elected representatives must rely upon huge bureaucracies hired from within their subjects. Often, the employees of such bureaucracies end up locking horns with the authorities when they perceive a discrepancy between their responsibilities and their financial remunerations.

The bureaucracies are huge in Eastern countries. Proportionately more people are on government payrolls in the East than the West, both at the federal (central) and state level. At the same time, elected officials and other decision-makers often find their hands tied as the revenues collected often fall short of the budgets needed to run the government. In part, this is a consequence of a lack of desire among the people to pay their taxes. When government salaries fail to keep up with the cost of living, the only option left for employees is to resort to a protest.

The people of East, generally speaking, are more dramatic and do not hesitate in acting out in the streets, especially when they perceive to have been slighted by the authorities. This results in confrontations that easily can turn violent, leading to shouting matches, fist-fighting, and hurling stones even at the security officers trying to break up the protest. The security people, in turn, do not hesitate to confront protesters with force. The use of crude and excessive force is not unusual. Hurling sticks without caring much as to where it hits and whom they hit is common on both sides of the protest line. With the privatization of the media, especially live-media, such scenes are easily projected all over the world.

This is not to say that this doesn't happen in the West. A good percentage of the Western people work in the private sectors and as such the government bureaucracies do not exert the kind of importance, as they do in the Eastern world. Raises in salaries are taken care of proactively on a routine basis in keeping with cost-of-living indices, thus avoiding the necessity for the employees to protest for their share of the pot. The government's coffers are not as limited as is often the case in Eastern countries, thanks to much greater wealth and a higher percentage of taxpayers who pay voluntarily or under penalty of the law. In fact, the revenues from taxes on properties and businesses are mandatory for everyone including the elites. While nobody on earth ever likes to pay taxes, and while each and every human being tries to find legal or illegal ways to avoid them, on the whole the pool of willing taxpayers is relatively large in the West.

In the West, should a discrepancy arise between the expectations of the employees and an unwillingness of the employers, a process of mediation is always available. And if that fails, certainly people can protest and even strike. But it is here that the difference between the West and the East becomes obvious.

The protests in the West are rarely loud, violent, or result in the kind of mayhem that we so often get to watch in the streets back home. The Westerners, most of the time, exhibit a rather toned-down behavior under such circumstances. One often watches a group of people quietly walking in fairly orderly rows and holding banners that explain their cause. The protestors also make sure that the ordinary public, the people not involved with the protest, are not affected. Even law enforcement agencies are not too much incited by such protests. However when protesters try to violate the law through non-violent civil disobedience, the law enforcement agencies use prescribed methods to detain the protesters, methods that require minimum necessary force to accomplish their tasks.

The concept of delivering a message through non-violence seems to have gradually been lost on the people belonging to the land of non-violence messiahs. If the purpose of the protest is simply to inform the authorities concerned, and if the ends could be achieved without violence and mayhem, why is there a need to interject violence into the protest?

While we are busy interrupting the functions of our highest legislative bodies of governments at both the central and state levels, the people of the West keep on finding ways to get the job done without unduly disrupting commerce or the government. While we keep on forcefully closing shops and businesses in support of some conflict almost every day somewhere in the country, the Western countries continue concentrating on the business of doing business seriously in order to stay in business and thus have an upper edge.

There is a dire need to turn our eyes toward the West and focus on a peaceful and disciplined way of protests. Hopefully this will project a better image of our people to the rest of the world, making it easier for us and our future generations to earn the respect that we rightfully deserve but that we seem to have lost in the mayhem of such protests.

36.

Western for Eight Hours,
Eastern for the Rest of the Day

Mankind from time immemorial has been motivated to explore new horizons. Such motivation stems from several factors. One of the main reasons is the natural quest in human beings to improve upon their economical and social lifestyles as well as of their future generations.

But beyond that, there always has been a need among all homo sapiens on this earth for the intellectual fulfillment through new knowledge, irrespective of their baseline perspectives. Such needs often motivate people from many cultures to leave their homelands without regard to their personal resources such as education or economical status and to look to far-away lands. Indians are no exception to this rule. When an opportunity knocks at the door, many decide to literally walk away from their homelands and their familiar surroundings. They leave their societies and their cultures behind and head for the unseen and untested waters of a new life on distant shores.

It is a fact of life that the native cultures get deeply ingrained in the psyche during the early developmental years of all human beings. Therefore, certain aspects of life, especially those to which one is exposed at an early age, are often difficult to change. After migrating to a different environment, a feeling of internal loss, albeit to a varying degree, lingers on for many years in the deeper layers of the minds of the immigrants. The expatriates always carry a sense of having lost something very special, something very near and dear to their hearts and emotional health. That 'something' is one's native culture. For a variety of reasons, one might not be able to define or express such loss and one may not be able to put it into succinct and comprehensive words, though it clearly exists. Recognition of this potential loss doesn't necessarily dawn upon people while they are still part and parcel of their inherited culture but on walking away, the loss shows and shows well.

After arriving in a new land ready to start a new life, many of the immigrants feel sandwiched like a piece of meat between two slices of bread, except that these slices happen to be two distinct cultures that are widely and diagonally apart. The Indian culture always guides human beings to continuously endeavor in seeking comforts for the soul in an un-witnessed next life, a life that supposedly gets activated only after one's permanent departure from this earth. Yet no living creature that ever roamed upon this earth has seen, participated in or witnessed such an experience, so claims the West. Such comforts and pleasures are mostly emphasized through abstract philosophies of Eastern religions, more than the Western beliefs.

The lifestyle in the West, on the other hand, is much more materialistic, catering to instant gratification. This indulgence in the Western lifestyle slowly and steadily starts penetrating into the well-established and deeply ingrained attitudes and behaviors of the people from the East. However, the degree of its modifying effects will depend upon several factors. They include but are not limited to one's prior mental development and maturity, understanding of their Eastern cultures, generalized awareness, education and the age at the time of arrival in the adopted country. The pressure in attempting to bring the sudden shift towards a new lifestyle from the well-established previous culture may lead to a mental as well as emotional hardship.

Regardless of how long one has lived in one's adopted homeland after leaving one's place of birth and one's culture, the immigrants always maintain a burning desire to fill such a vacuum created by this change. They try to surround themselves with people and environments that are similar to the ones that they had left behind. Here I am reminded of an incident that underlines my point:

A person from India who had lived all his life in a relatively remote village landed in a German city where some of his hometown friends had earlier migrated. The friends took him to the place where they were staying. Night came, but this person was not able to sleep, awakening again and again. Night after night his restlessness kept him deprived of sleep. Watching his helplessness, one of the friends hesitatingly mentioned that he too had experienced difficulties when he arrived. This friend explained to the newly-arrived guest that the difficulty in falling asleep was the consequence of extreme degree of quietness of the background, to which he was not accustomed back home. Adding noise-filled Indian music in the background helped the recent arrival to go back to sleep.

The point here is that "The environments in which one grows up, leaves imprints on one's subconscious mind!

Members of immigrant communities often live double lives as a consequence of previous experiences that are in direct contrast and, often, conflict with the lifestyles of their adopted homelands. In order to create some semblance of stability in their lives, they try to build an artificial partition within their mental framework. The attitudes and behaviors they display during the working eight hours of the day can be entirely different from the ones they have within the boundaries of their homes or within the context of their social lives.

Arriving at work, the immigrants become immersed in the culture of the adopted homeland and for obvious reasons. They talk and speak the language of the land. They intermingle with co-workers and act and behave like their peers for the most part, as they should. Come lunch time, they all go out to eat like everyone else. As they try to integrate their behaviors into the norms of their new environments, their colleagues at work are often not in positions to judge, understand or even have any awareness of the extreme metamorphosis that many of them end up going through every day, day in and day out.

As the day comes to a close, the immigrants turn the page and open up a new chapter of the book of their lives. Their attitudes and expectations revert back to the cultures and lifestyles that they were used to earlier. Given a choice, nearly all immigrants would like to eat the food that they were used to, dress like they were used to, and talk like they were used to. They will often socialize with friends and relatives from their country rather than people from their new country and culture. Their get-togethers at homes are geared to their own kinds of people in their own styles. Celebrations of back-home festivals and holidays are eagerly anticipated, and they are performed with even more gusto than what was done back home. Like an oasis in a desert, whenever and wherever they find another family of their kind, they often tend to flock towards it.

The immigrants suddenly become more religious than ever before or at least they try to make their fellow immigrants believe that they have become so. Oftentimes, many among them attempt to become leaders of their immigrant communities, whether through leadership in religious places or through whatever else comes their way. Suddenly, everyone tries to metamorphose and pose as the most important and highly sought after person in their communities, usually with an 'I am better than anyone else' attitude.

In a nutshell, after being done with the 'Western thing' for eight-hour day at the office or any other work site for earning a living, immigrants attempt hard to revert back and merge into their previous identities and lifestyles. Like a lotus flower, they exist, live and grow within the 'muddy waters,' yet try to stay aloof and not get wet. Is this good or bad?

The answers to such questions are difficult to come by. In fact, many among the immigrants may not even be following such a pattern. They seem to have come to a conclusion that sooner or later, their Western-born children are going to assimilate and become part of the Western culture anyway. So where is the need and why? In a way, they attempt to make the job of assimilation easy but again that may not necessarily be compatible or true to their inner voice.

I, for one, believe that the weight of the cultural baggage that Eastern immigrants bring with them is far too heavy and it may continue to impose itself upon their psyche for a while. To minimize this pain, there is a need for them to find ways to maintain a cultural balance between their native and adopted lifestyles and culture. Hopefully, one day the Western majority will come to realize, understand and appreciate the dilemma of Eastern immigrants and attempt to extend them a helping hand. In accepting some differences in the mental make-up of these newly arrived Westerners-to-be, the native-born will have to keep on showing reasonable amount of resilience in their understanding. Through this generosity of the indigenous people, the immigrants will also be then able to gain a piece of the cultural pie in the land that they have decided to live in.

This way the immigrants will be able to enjoy their lives peacefully with all the blessings that this great land of the West has to offer. Gradually, the immigrants while maintaining their love-affair with the cultures of the lands of their births, will slowly become equal and proud partners in the culture that they have come to adopt.

37.

Alcohol Abuse
Discriminates Between Sexes

When I thought of writing on this sensitive issue, the consequences of such an undertaking were fairly obvious to me. In this kind of endeavor, one could inadvertently cross a fine line and open oneself to being labeled a 'Male Chauvinist.' Yet I felt imperative to highlight the ill-effects of habitual drinking upon the so-called Bharatiyaa-Naari, or the Indian Woman, as well as on the other women of the Indian subcontinent, given the fact that such awareness among the diaspora is less than adequate. The adverse effects of habitual drinking are far more injurious to the fairer sex than to their male counterparts. The well-informed and educated woman might simply consider this writing an unnecessary and unwanted sermon. However, not all of us come in contact with pertinent scientific medical literature in relation to this topic, hence the need for such a write up.

Times were, especially in the Eastern cultures, when most women didn't get into the habit of drinking alcohol in any way, shape or form. Drinking for women was a taboo and was limited to a very few of the so-called "economically well-placed" families. As times changed, so did habits and cultures. The world kept on getting smaller and dissemination of information became easy. Western culture, being dominant in its appeal, readily took upon the lead in all what was good or bad while others simply followed suit.

Consequently, some modern Indian women, especially those who belonged to the Diaspora, felt compelled to initiate or adopt this so-called culturally acceptable habit. This could well have been due, in part, to an internal desire that they kept suppressed voluntarily or as a consequence of circumstances that were out of their control, one of them being a subtle encouragement from their life partners. Drinking induced a sense of God-sent pseudo-liberation and reprieve from an age-old repression of the "Fair-Sex" that has been in vogue in Eastern societies. This behavior also brought about a feeling of equality as well as camaraderie and over a period of time some women started considering such unhealthy indulgences as their rights. Unfortunately they didn't prepare themselves for all the eventualities, known or not, that could befall upon them and their families with incessant indulgence.

Women on the whole, by no means have surpassed men in so far this undesirable habit is concerned. Even now, various surveys reveal that women are only half as likely as men in terms of their numbers and dependence upon alcohol. Yet it is important for our women-folks to realize that they are intrinsically more vulnerable to the ill-effects of alcohol simply because their body organs are more likely to sustain damage as compared to men with an intake of equal amount of alcohol. And this I say, not out of discrimination but because physiologically, a woman's body has a higher percentage of fat and a lower percentage of water.

Such a ratio causes less dilution of alcohol with resultant more ill-effects. A woman who is the same size as a man shows the ill effects of alcohol more quickly and strongly. With the same amount of alcohol intake, the blood level in a woman rises a third higher and it takes a third longer to eliminate. A young man's liver takes one hour to process one drink whereas a similar drink will take a third longer in a woman. It should be noted, however, that gender-specific genetic factors leading to differential sensitivities in two sexes are not yet clearly defined. They are being aggressively looked at in various animal studies.

Cirrhosis of the liver and alcoholic hepatitis develops in a shorter time and with the use of less alcohol. Likewise, mal-nourishment in women comes quickly. Alcohol has also been described as another important risk factor for breast cancer in women, again proving the fact that "drinking hits a woman hard where it hurts the most." The incidence rises if a woman smokes concomitantly and uses contraceptives. Osteoporosis, or thinning of the bones, is another consequence of heavy drinking in women and comes with an increased incidence of fractures.

Magnetic resonance imaging (MRI) has shown that a woman's brain, especially the part concerned with multiple functions, is more vulnerable to the ill-effects of alcohol than that of a man. Pound per pound, women are more susceptible to suffer from alcohol-related damage to heart muscles, causing what is often known as cardiomyopathy in medical terminology. With alcohol, the pancreas is also damaged more in women than men. More information about drinking-related health concerns in women and men is available in the Alcohol Policies Project fact sheet issued by the Center for Science in the Public interest.

Some woman might believe that drinking enhances their sex drive but it is just a belief rather than fact. Drinking per se doesn't enhance the libido rather young women who drink usually end up having early sexual experiences, either consensual or against their will, and that too with a greater number of partners. The report "Are women more vulnerable to Alcohol's Effects?" Issued by the National Institute on Alcohol Abuse and Alcoholism, published in Alcoholism 1999, clearly states that women alcoholics are more susceptible to interpersonal violence and traffic accidents. With similar levels of alcohol concentration in blood, women have a higher risk of driver-deaths than men.

Although statistics for alcohol use in women have been well-known for Western women, such information about Asian women in general and Indian women in particular is sketchy. But it seems that Asian women are gradually catching up in numbers. A perusal of recent surveys in the U.K. has brought forth conflicting incidence amongst different communities of Asians. In one Internet report, the alcohol use in Pakistani women is 10% whereas in Bengali women it is about 17%. In Hindu women, the incidence is about 20% while Sikh women stand atop with a 25% incidence.

It is important to realize that drinking does not need to be used by 'Fair Sex' as a tool in seeking equality with men. There are many more positive avenues through which this can be achieved. At the same time, I hope that this write up in any way, shape or form is not construed as a license authorizing men to take up habitual drinking for that will be the farthest from my intent.

38.
Ownership of Domestic Servants

Once upon a time, a Russian, born and raised in Russia where existence of God is often denied, happened to visit India for the first time. He was perplexed by what he saw. Watching all the haphazardness in every facet of the daily Indian life, he simply couldn't figure out how exactly India keeps going amidst all the chaos.

After being in India for a few days, he emphatically mentioned to his hosts about his desire to change his long-held belief about the non-existence of God. He stated, "We, the citizens of communist Russia must have been wrong all along about such a belief. Isn't it amazing that no efforts are being spared by your politicians and ordinary people in ripping their own country apart and letting it go down the drain, yet life in India moves haltingly forward? Such a system should have completely torn apart India's political and social fabric long ago. I am convinced that some occult higher power – a so-called God -- must be standing guard in order to keep India on track, protecting it from itself and all the evil that you people are incessantly unleashing on your motherland." What a truth!

Given a close scrutiny, it seems that we have been a failure in carrying out our duties according to the age-old spiritual wisdom imparted to us by our ancestors, seers, and sages. Looking into any aspect of modern life, one finds abundant examples of a twisted sense of truthful living. We have lost the essential ingredients of a morally correct life. We have forgotten or ignored the ideals of honest work that ensures a comfortable yet simple life that maintains a concern about the needs of others. We are living our lives in such a selfish manner that most of our efforts involve finding ways to avoid hard and honest work.

Taking advantage of the labor of the others, through means that might not be ethical, is a norm. We take pride in actions that could be considered clearly wrong, both spiritually and socially, especially if understood from the viewpoints of people belonging to non-Indian cultures. Yet we do not care what others think and simply keep on moving in a direction that lets our country and culture go down the drain

This write up focuses on just one aspect of our lost ideals; the apparent necessity of having what an Indian back home would often perceive as 'ownership' of domestic servants.

Our ancestors often tried to announce their elevated social status through ownership of the heads of cattle. Nowadays the presence of household servants among some middle class Indians is considered an enhancement of their social status in the eyes of relatives and friends. Oftentimes it might not be based on a true need. This phenomenon among middle class Indians has become contagious and indeed a true menace. Yet, by having servants around, we only emphasize and exaggerate our laziness in most of the circumstances.

During one of our visits to India, my wife and I were invited to lunch at the house of a relative. A refrigerator containing cold bottles of water was located a couple of feet away from where the host's wife was sitting at the dining table. A young Nepalese boy named Bahadur (a common name amongst many Nepalese), not more than twelve years of age, was employed as a domestic servant in the household of our hosts. He was working in the kitchen that was at least fifty feet away, if not more, from the dining table.

The lady of the house wanted to offer water to us, so she started shouting aloud, *"Bahadur! Arey! Fridge se thunda paani laauo, thunda,"* or "Bahadur! Come and fetch cold water bottles from the refrigerator and serve." We felt embarrassed, as it was totally unfair to bother a person, even if that happens to be a servant, at fifty or sixty feet away when what we needed was easily approachable by the lady of the house without even getting up from her chair. My wife stood up and tried to extend her arm to take a bottle from the refrigerator. The lady of the house said, "This is not your job, *Bhainji!* We have a servant at our house. Let him take care of it."

It was all too obvious that such an attitude on our hostess's part was simply an indirect attempt to inform us that she was not only in a position to own a servant, but she indeed had one. At this point, I started mentioning the advantages of indulging oneself in the minor physical chores of the house. By avoiding dependence upon the servants, she was informed, she could control her weight, which was somewhat generous to begin with, and also help lower her blood pressure, for which she was under a doctor's care. During my later visit with the same family some years later, it was all too obvious that my unsolicited medical advice had fallen upon deaf ears, for the lady of the house appeared to have doubled her size.

It must be said that the lady's health appeared to have declined further, so much so that she truly needed domestic help now. Too much dependence, even for routine domestic chores, might have played a role here, in part.

There is a need to emphasize that as a community, we often try to ignore or even degrade the people belonging to lower socio-economical strata. We perceive ownership of domestic servants to be a privilege while ignoring the underlying reality that it is neither worthy of pride nor healthy. At times, the household servants are underage boys and girls, sometimes even younger than 12 years of age, and invariably belonging to the poorest of the poor families of Eastern Uttar Pradesh, Bihar or Nepal.

They arrive to work at the homes of their masters at an age when they have barely opened their eyes to the complexities of the world. Like little birds, they are made to fly away from the nests of their families often against their will. And like little helpless animals, they are put to work from sunrise to sunset, and often later. They end up existing in this cruel world at the mercy of their masters who, instead of being shameful for their behaviors, display pride in owning them outright and in using them for all of their household chores.

Many times they are made to survive on the leftover food from the plates of their owners. They are usually relegated to exist in a remote nook of the backyard of the house in a makeshift hut that is proudly labeled as the servant's quarter. They are asked to dress with the used clothing of the family members. They are often 'on the job' twenty-four hours a day, every day of the week. The impression is often projected that these little child-slaves have been bought outright and are somehow the "children of a lesser God." Obviously, I do not claim that such is always true.

We boast of having many laws on the books against the exploitation of the helpless and the poor, yet we end up ignoring the plight of these poor young children-turned-servants. The books in which these laws were written keep on collecting dust somewhere on the shelves of bureaucracy.

Another strange perspective from an entirely different angle was brought forth during my discussion with that family. The hostess happened to mention in passing that by providing a job to the domestic servant, she was not merely helping herself, but also doing a favor to the poverty-stricken family of little 'Bahadur.' She did seem to have a point, but to me it only made sense if a child was of a legal working age and was treated in a humane way without any exploitation. But this may not be the case always.

Understanding valuable and morally correct customs of Western culture can provide us with an opportunity to recognize the anomalies in our culture that may need to be highlighted and explained to our near and dear ones when we find an occasion to do so. In this way, the value and dignity of self-help can be reinforced and perhaps headway can be made with a possibility of causing a dent in the age-old, yet not-so-ethical labor practices. Only through personal contacts on one to one basis, can one make inroads into such style of living and thwart the progression of this unfortunate menace. However, this is not to say that each and every cultural aspect of the West is above board.

Creating laws that require and force keepers of domestic servants to arrange and support part-time schooling of their wards, in addition to looking after their health and other needs, will be a step in the right direction. Establishment of child protective agencies, if not established already, would keep a watch upon those who try to infringe upon human rights of the children. It will assist and protect many helpless children from being exploited while letting those concerned with their status have their desires fulfilled, but this time through honest and lawful means.